Sew Decorative

QUICK AND EASY HOME ACCENTS
from *SEW NEWS*

By the Editors of

sewNEWS
the trusted sewing source

Martingale ®
& COMPANY

sewNEWS
the trusted sewing source

Sew Decorative: Quick and Easy Home Accents
from *Sew News*
© 2011 by the Editors of *Sew News* Magazine

Published by Martingale & Company®.
That Patchwork Place® is an imprint of
Martingale & Company.

Martingale & Company
19021 120th Ave. NE, Suite 102
Bothell, WA 98011-9511 USA
www.martingale-pub.com

CREDITS

President & CEO: Tom Wierzbicki
Editor in Chief: Mary V. Green
Managing Editor: Tina Cook
Design Director: Stan Green
Developmental Editor: Karen Costello Soltys
Production Manager: Regina Girard
Technical Editor: Christine Barnes
Copy Editor: Marcy Heffernan
Illustrator: Laurel Strand
Cover & Text Designer: Stan Green
Photographer: Joe Hancock Studio

Sew News, ISSN 0273-8120, is published bimonthly by Creative Crafts Group, LLC, 741 Corporate Circle, Suite A, Golden, CO 80401, www.sewnews.com.

Printed in China
16 15 14 13 12 11   8 7 6 5 4 3 2 1

Library of Congress Cataloging-in-Publication Data
is available upon request.

ISBN: 978-1-60468-025-6

MISSION STATEMENT
Dedicated to providing quality products and service to inspire creativity.

CONTENTS

Introduction ❖ 4

Dining in Style ❖ 5

    Chain-Stitched Table Runner 7

    Table for Two 13

    Patchwork Place Mats 15

    Patchwork Pot Holders 17

    Outdoor Table Setting 21

    Tucked Place Mats 25

    Tie Table Runner 31

Custom Bed and Bath ❖ 34

    Trim Time 35

    Designer Sheet and Pillowcases 41

    Skirting the Issue 43

    Room with a View 47

    Bathroom Organizer 51

    Embellished Lampshade 55

    Lamp of Luxury 56

    Lounge Sack 59

Pillow Power ❖ 64

    Eastern Influence 65

    Graphic Pillows 67

    Buttoned and Basic Pillows 71

    Sunroom Seating 73

    Gather 'Round 78

    Connect the Dots 81

    Cube Pillow 82

    Shirred Pillows 85

    Envelope Pillow 89

Home-Sewing Specifications ❖ 92

Project Contributors ❖ 96

Introduction

What makes a house a home? The fabulous decor, of course!

Sewing your own custom decor is the best way to express your personal style throughout your home. Whether your style is contemporary, country, retro, or rustic, it's much easier to coordinate accessories when you're able to choose the fabric, trim, and embellishments yourself. Maybe you're starting from scratch, with bare walls and plain furniture. Or your home may need an update into the twenty-first century. Perhaps you're converting one room into an office or nursery. Or it could be time for a few new pillows and curtains. Whatever the reason, there are many affordable options in the pages of this book.

Adding new pillows is the most inexpensive way to update a room. Plus, a pillow is a great beginner project. Choose from myriad closure options, including zippers, buttons, loops, and folds, and experiment with stitching techniques like embroidery, shirring, and reverse appliqué. In under an hour, and with less than one yard of fabric, your pillow needs will be met. Turn to "Pillow Power" (page 64) to see just how easy it is!

Table runners, place mats, napkins, and pot holders are other great projects for beginners. But you can also take them to the next level and create something truly exquisite, as they're great canvases to showcase beautiful stitching and intricate detailing. People say that you eat with your eyes first. I believe that this begins with the table decor and ends with the food presentation. "Dining in Style" (facing page) will inspire you to set the mood with a fabric feast before serving family and guests your culinary delights.

Let's not forget the bedroom and bathroom. Continual updates to your safe havens will stimulate your creativity *and* help you relax. Rickrack-trimmed sheets and a comfy lounge sack may be just what you need to cozy up in your bedroom retreat. A shower organizer fashioned from two towels can turn you into a morning person. Evaluate your needs and rejuvenate your senses with "Custom Bed and Bath" (page 34) as your guide.

No big-box store carries everything you need to make your house your home. The style you express, the mood you evoke, and the memories you create cannot be left to chance. Start small with a simple pillow project, or go big with a massive room makeover. Before you know it, you'll be living in a newly renovated space that didn't require drywall and paint or create construction dust!

Happy sewing,
Ellen March
Sew News Editor

DINING IN STYLE

Setting a beautiful table really begins with what goes under the dishes, and for every dining occasion there is a runner, place mat, or innovative table covering to serve as the backdrop for a memorable meal. Sew crisp white linens and embroider them using simple stitches and fresh colors, or stitch bright place mats from indoor-outdoor fabrics. An embellished cashmere scarf and a runner fashioned from cast-off ties add a distinctive touch. Oh, and don't forget the time-honored pot holder; after all, you'll need to bring that delicious food to the table!

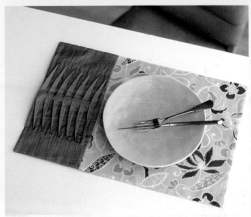

Chain-Stitched TABLE RUNNER

Welcome spring to your table with a runner, place mats, and napkins that show off brightly colored hand embroidery. These projects are perfect for practicing the chain stitch and French knots. The embroidery is so easy you'll want to create a set for each season.

Designed by Kate Bashynski

You'll Need

Yardages are based on 42"-wide or wider fabric. Materials listed will make two 14" x 14" napkins, two 14" x 20" place mats, and one 16" x 36" table runner.

- 1⅞ yards of washable linen or cotton/linen fabric
- Template material
- Matching all-purpose thread
- *Or* purchased table runner, place mats, and napkins
- Acrylic ruler with marked grid
- Water-soluble fabric-marking pen
- 4 colors of embroidery thread or floss
- Hand-embroidery needles (see step 1, page 8)
- 6" to 8" embroidery hoop
- Spray starch (optional)

Preparation

Prewash the fabric or the purchased linens following the manufacturer's instructions. Apply spray starch to add crispness to the fabric if desired. If you're using purchased linens, skip to "Embroidery Instructions" on page 8.

Cutting

From the linen fabric, cut:
2 squares, 17½" x 17½"
2 rectangles, 17½" x 23½"
1 rectangle, 19½" x 39½"

Sewing Instructions

The instructions that follow are for the napkins; repeat for the place mats and table runner.

1. Trace the mitered corner guide (page 11) onto template material; cut out the template.
2. Position the template at each fabric corner and trace the cutting lines.

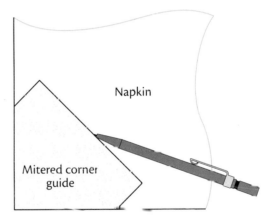

Napkin

Mitered corner guide

3. Cut out each corner shape.

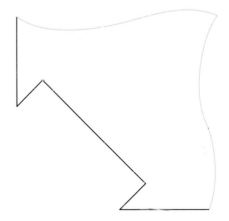

4. With right sides together, fold the fabric diagonally so the corner cutouts are folded in half. Align the cut edges and pin the layers together.

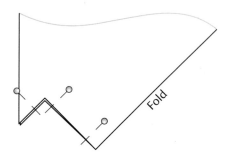

5. Stitch ¼" from the cut corner edges to form the mitered corner. When you approach the corner, shorten the stitch length (1.5 to 2.0 mm). Stop stitching at the corner, lower the needle into the fabric, and lift the presser foot to pivot the fabric. Align the fabric to continue stitching ¼" from the adjacent cut edge, lower the presser foot, and continue stitching. Cut the thread tails and press the stitched areas flat.

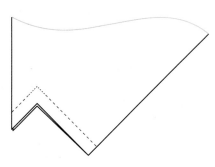

6. Clip into each corner, being careful not to cut the stitching.

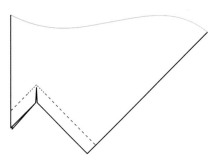

7. Finger-press the seam allowances open. Press the raw edges ½" toward the wrong side to begin forming the hem. Turn the napkin right side out; a 1¼" hem will naturally form on the wrong side. Press again.

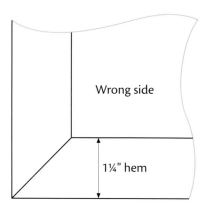

8. Machine stitch close to the first pressed edge using a straight stitch or a narrow blanket stitch.

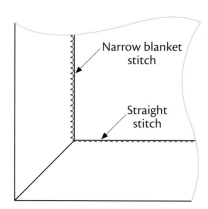

Embroidery Instructions

1. Select a hand-embroidery needle by testing the ease of threading the needle with the embroidery thread or floss; then pass the threaded needle through a scrap of fabric. The threaded needle should enter and exit the fabric smoothly. You shouldn't have to struggle when threading the needle or taking stitches.

2. Mark the stitching lines on the fabric right side with dots. Mark two adjacent edges on each napkin, one or both short ends on each place mat, and all four edges on the table runner. The chain-stitched rows on the featured linens are spaced ½" apart, with ¼" spacing between the dots.

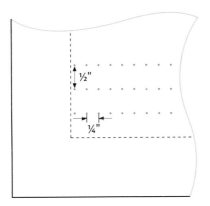

The French knot rows on the featured table runner are centered between the chain-stitched rows, with ½" spacing between the dots.

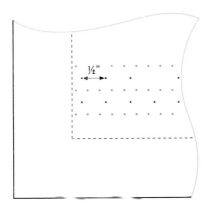

The napkins have French knots only in the corner grid created by the chain-stitched rows.

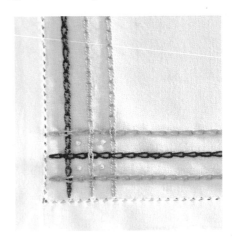

3. Hoop the fabric in the embroidery hoop, near a corner. The fabric should be taut and smooth but not stretched or distorted.

4. Cut the lengths of embroidery thread or floss approximately 12" to 18". (Longer lengths can tangle easily and will show abrasion damage caused by the repeated entering and exiting through the fabric.) Chain stitch the rows within the hoop area first, and then add the French knots at each dot marking. See "Embroidery How-To" (pages 10 and 11) for chain stitching and French knot instructions. Rehoop the fabric as needed to complete the embroidery.

5. When you finish the embroidery, remove any visible marking before pressing the project. The heat of an iron can permanently set some marking pen and pencil marks.

6. Gently press the completed table linens right side down on a padded surface to prevent flattening the stitches.

EMBROIDERY HOW-TO

Chain stitch: Knot the thread. Bring the embroidery thread or floss up from the fabric wrong side at 1 (the first dot mark in the corner of the work). Make a loop to the left, holding the loop with your left thumb. Insert the needle at 2 and bring it up at 3. Pull the needle and thread through the loop, but not too tightly.

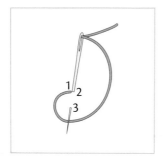

Repeat by inserting the needle inside the first loop at 4 and back up at 5. Continue until the entire row of dots is covered. End by inserting the needle at the bottom of the last stitch; knot the thread on the wrong side.

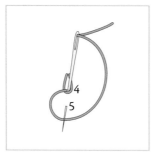

French knot: Knot the thread. Bring the needle up through the fabric at 1. Holding the embroidery thread or floss with your other hand, wrap it around the needle three times.

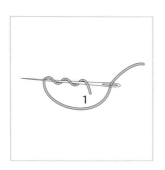

Fresh colors and simple stitches decorate crisp table linens.

Gently pulling the thread taut with your fingers, insert the needle down at 2, right next to 1. Pull the thread through to the fabric wrong side, maintaining the tension on the thread with your fingers until the knot rests securely on the fabric surface. Move the needle to the next dot and form another French knot. Continue until the row of dots is covered. End by knotting the thread after bringing the needle to the fabric wrong side.

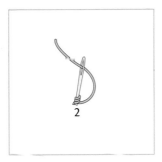

To reduce hoop marks, remove the embroidery from the hoop overnight or for any extended period of time when you won't be stitching. This allows the fabric and the embroidery to relax from the hoop pressure.

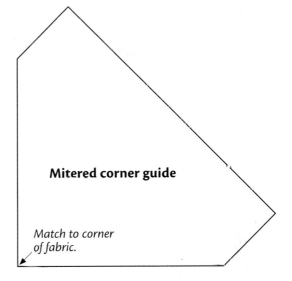

Mitered corner guide

Match to corner of fabric.

TABLE for TWO

Add a personal touch to a cashmere scarf for a luxurious table runner. Strips of solid-colored fabric, fused to the scarf, form the backdrop for floral or other motifs.

Designed by Shannon Dennis

You'll Need

Yardages are based on 42"-wide fabric.

- ¾ yard of solid-colored fabric
- ⅜ yard of print with large design elements, such as flowers, for appliqué
- 2 packages (5 sheets each) of double-sided fusible-web sheets
- Rotary cutter, ruler, and mat
- Cashmere scarf
- Water-soluble fabric-marking pen
- Pressing sheet
- Silver or gold metallic thread
- Lightweight bobbin thread
- Size 90/14 topstitching needle
- Crystals, pearls, or beads (optional)

Instructions

1. Peel off one side of one fusible-web sheet. Leave the other side intact. Place the sticky side down on the wrong side of the solid-colored fabric. Press with a dry iron.
2. Using the rotary equipment, cut the fusible-backed fabric into 1"-wide strips.
3. Measure 8" to 10" from each scarf end and draw a line using the marking pen. Trim the fabric strips and arrange them as desired within the marked areas. The strips shown here were separated a bit to allow the scarf to show through.
4. Peel away the remaining paper from each strip to expose the adhesive. With the sticky side down on the scarf, fuse the strips in place using a pressing sheet and steam for a permanent hold.
5. Peel off one side of another fusible-web sheet and place the sticky side down on the print wrong side. Press with a dry iron. Cut out several large design motifs, such as flowers or leaves. Remove the remaining paper from each design. Position and fuse the motifs to the strips in a random pattern.
6. Using metallic thread, randomly straight stitch or free-motion stitch over the strips and motifs.

SEW SMART
Use a size 90/14 topstitching needle and lightweight bobbin thread for best results when sewing with fragile metallic thread.

7. Add crystals, pearls, or beads to the runner for embellishment, if desired.

Patchwork PLACE MATS

Try your hand at patchwork piecing by making these cool place mats. Use coordinating cotton fabrics; they work well for patchwork and are easy to launder. Mix and match the widths of each strip based on the prints you want to feature. Try a combination of prints and solid fabrics for a modern look.

Designed by Linda Permann

You'll Need

Yardages are based on 42"-wide fabric.
Materials listed make two 15" x 20" place mats.

- 1 yard of Japanese linen or dobby fabric for front and back
- 15 to 20 assorted coordinating fabric scraps, each at least 2" x 6", for patchwork
- Two 16" x 21" rectangles of quilt batting
- Rotary cutter, ruler, and mat
- Matching all-purpose thread

SEW SMART

Because place mats require frequent laundering, prewash your fabrics according to the manufacturer's instructions.

Instructions

1. From the linen, cut two 16" x 21" rectangles, two 13¼" x 16" rectangles, and two 2¾" x 16" strips. Set aside.
2. Cut the coordinating scraps into 6"-long pieces, varying the widths from 2" to 5" according to your preference.
3. Arrange the pieces in a pleasing order until they measure approximately 19" vertically. Make a mental note or snap a digital photo of the arrangement.

4. Position the first two pieces right sides together. Stitch one long edge using a ¼" seam allowance. Join the third and fourth pieces in the same manner. Repeat to join the remaining pairs. If you have an uneven number of pieces, stitch the remaining piece to the lower edge of the last pair. Press the seam allowances down.

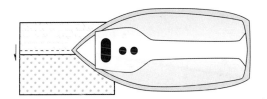

PIECE BY PIECE

To vary the design lines, combine two different small fabric pieces to make a 6"-wide patchwork strip.

5. Stitch the pairs together using a ¼" seam allowance to make one long patchwork strip. Press the seam allowances downward. Trim the strip to 16" long.

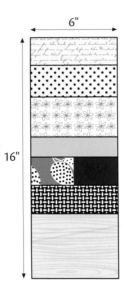

6. With right sides together, pin one 2¾" x 16" linen or dobby strip to the patchwork-strip right edge. Stitch using a ¼" seam allowance. Press the seam allowances toward the linen strip.

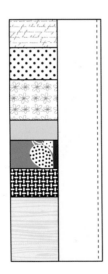

7. Pin and stitch one 13¼" x 16" rectangle to the patchwork-strip left edge in the same manner.

8. Position a 16" x 21" linen rectangle right side up over a batting rectangle. Place the patchwork rectangle right side down on top of the layers, aligning all the edges. Pin the layers. Stitch around the two short edges and one long edge using a ½" seam allowance. Clip the corners to reduce the bulk.

9. Turn right side out and press, turning under the seam allowances at the opening; pin.

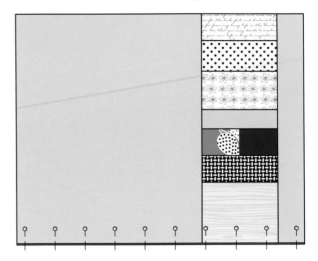

10. Topstitch the linen along each patchwork-strip edge. Topstitch around the place-mat perimeter, making sure to catch the opening edges. Repeat steps 1–10 to make the second place mat.

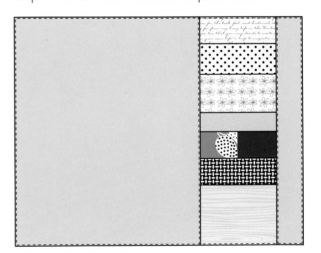

Patchwork POT HOLDERS

These cheerful pot holders made of scraps perk up a tired kitchen in no time at all. For your safety, be sure to use at least one layer of heat-proof batting, such as Insul-Bright, which is heat-resistant up to 400°F.

Designed by Linda Permann

You'll Need

Materials listed will make two 8½" square pot holders.

- ◆ Assorted fat quarters or fabric scraps
- ◆ Two 9" squares of Insul-Bright batting
- ◆ Two 9" squares of cotton batting (polyester might melt)
- ◆ Matching all-purpose thread
- ◆ Point turner

Cutting

From the fat quarters and scraps for *each* pot holder, cut:

2 squares, 4¾" x 4¾"
1 strip, 1" x 9"
1 strip, 1½" x 9"
1 strip, 3¼" x 9"
1 square for backing, 9" x 9"
1 strip for hanging loop, 2" x 7"

Instructions

Use ¼" seam allowances unless otherwise noted.

1. With right sides together, stitch the two 4¾" squares along one edge. Press the seam allowances to one side. With right sides together, stitch the 1" x 9" strip to the lower edge of the pieced squares; press the seam allowances toward the strip. Add the 1½"-wide strip and the 3¼"-wide strip in the same manner, pressing the seam allowances downward. Repeat for the second pot holder.

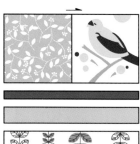
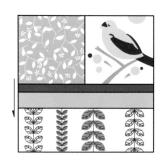

2. To make each hanging loop, fold one long edge of a 2" x 7" strip ½" toward the wrong side; press. Repeat with the other long edge. Fold the strip in half lengthwise; press. Stitch along the folded edges.

3. Layer the pieces as follows: cotton batting, Insul-Bright batting, patchwork square (right side up), backing square (wrong side up). Fold the hanging loop in half; position it between the two fabric layers, ¾" from one corner.

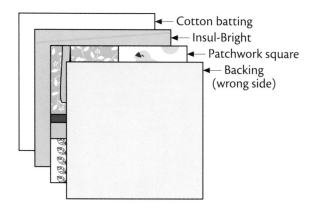

Cotton batting
Insul-Bright
Patchwork square
Backing (wrong side)

4. Pin the layers together. Stitch around the potholder perimeter, pivoting at the corners and leaving a 6" opening on the bottom edge for turning. Carefully clip both batting squares as close to the stitching line as possible. Clip the corners to reduce the bulk.

5. Turn the pot holder right side out and use the point turner to smooth the corners; press. Turn under the seam allowances at the opening, trimming the batting as necessary to achieve a smooth seam; pin. Topstitch around the potholder perimeter, making sure to catch the opening edges.

6. With the pot holder facing up, topstitch just above the horizontal seams. Topstitch down the center, slightly to the left of the pieced-squares seam.

A bright backing fabric makes the pot holders pretty on both sides.

Topstitching adds a tailored touch and secures the layers of fabric and batting.

Outdoor TABLE SETTING

Stitch a cheery and practical outdoor table setting using fabrics that stand up to the elements. Outdoor fabric, such as Sunbrella, is ideal because it's substantial; washable; fast drying; and stain-, fade-, and mildew-resistant. Cute pockets keep napkins and plastic utensils from blowing away on a breezy day.

Designed by Debbie Homer

You'll Need

Yardages are based on 54"- or 60"-wide fabric. Materials listed will make four 14" x 20" place mats and one 14" x 60" table runner

- 1⅞ yards of orange solid fabric for runner
- 1⅛ yards of yellow solid fabric for place-mat backing
- 1 yard of multicolored striped fabric for place-mat front
- ½ yard of lime green–and–white striped fabric* for place-mat and runner pockets
- Rotary cutter, ruler, and mat
- Air-soluble fabric marker
- All-purpose lime green thread
- Knitting needle

* *Fabric must be printed on both sides.*

Cutting

From the yellow solid fabric, cut:
4 rectangles, 17" x 23"

From the multicolored striped fabric, cut:
4 rectangles, 14" x 20"

From the orange solid fabric, cut:
2 rectangles, 15" x 61"

From the lime green–and–white striped fabric, cut
4 rectangles, 6" x 9"
2 rectangles, 7½" x 12"

Place-Mat Instructions

Use ½" seam allowances unless otherwise noted.

1. With wrong sides together, position the 14" x 20" striped rectangle over the 17" x 23" yellow rectangle so 1½" of backing shows around each outer edge.

2. To create a border from the backing fabric, fold one backing lower edge forward 1½" over the place-mat lower edge. Fold the backing corner at a 45° angle.

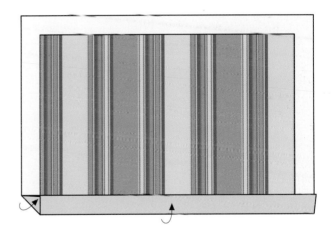

> ### PRESSING MATTERS
> Don't iron Sunbrella fabric unless your iron has a Teflon plate. If it does, use a very low heat setting.

3. Fold the backing side edge forward 1½" to create a mitered-corner effect; pin. Repeat for the other three corners.

4. Set your machine for an overcast stitch and experiment on a fabric scrap. Overcast the backing raw edges and diagonally along the mitered-corner folds. Finger-press the edges.

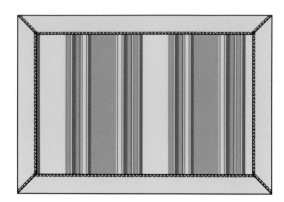

5. To create the pocket, fold the 6" x 9" fabric rectangle in half lengthwise, right sides together. Designate one short end as the lower edge. Mark the long open edges 2½" up from the lower edge. Draw a diagonal line connecting the mark to the lower folded edge. With the rectangle still folded, cut along the line.

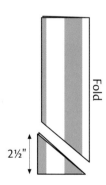

Fold

2½"

6. Unfold the pocket and fold the pocket upper edge 2" toward the fabric right side; finger-press. Overcast the raw edge.

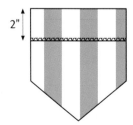

2"

7. Position the pocket right side up on the place mat so the lower point and right edge are ¼" from the overcast border edges; pin. Overcast the pocket edges. Repeat to make the remaining place mats.

Table-Runner Instructions

Use ½" seam allowances unless otherwise noted.

1. To create the pointed ends on the runner, fold one 15" x 61" rectangle in half lengthwise, right sides together. At one end, mark the long open edges 6" up from the lower edge. Draw a diagonal line connecting the mark to the lower folded edge.

2. With the fabric still folded, cut along the line. Repeat at the other end of the rectangle. Repeat on the remaining 15" x 61" rectangle.

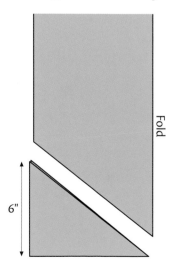

Fold

6"

3. To create the pocket, fold one 7½" x 12" rectangle in half lengthwise, right sides together. Designate one short edge as the lower edge. Mark the long open edges 3" up from the lower edge. Draw a diagonal line connecting the mark to the lower folded edge. With the rectangle still folded, cut along the line.

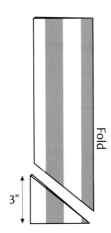

Fold

3"

4. Unfold the pocket and fold one pocket upper edge 3" toward the fabric right side; finger-press. Overcast the raw edge. Repeat to create the remaining pocket.

5. Position one pocket right side up on one runner piece, vertically centered, with the pocket point 3" from the runner point; pin

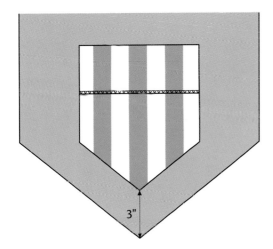

3"

6. Overcast the pocket edges. Repeat to stitch the remaining pocket to the opposite end of the runner piece.

7. With right sides together, pin the runner pieces through both layers. Stitch around the perimeter using a ½" seam allowance, pivoting at the corners and points and leaving a 6" opening along one edge for turning. Trim the points to reduce the bulk.

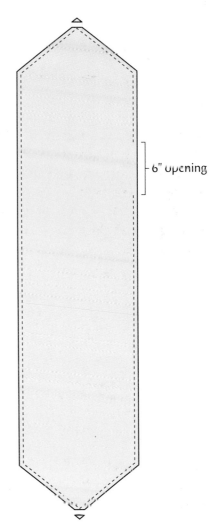

6" opening

8. Turn the runner right side out. Use the knitting needle to push out the seams and corners. Finger-press the edges.

9. Turn under the seam allowances at the opening; finger-press. Topstitch the runner using a ⅜" seam allowance, making sure to catch the opening edges.

Tucked PLACE MATS

Functional place mats are a staple of casual dining—and a great showcase for your creativity. Combine pressed folds and straight stitches to make these eye-catching table accessories.

Designed by Kate Bashynski

You'll Need

Yardages are based on 42"-wide fabric
Materials listed will make two 12" x 18" place mats.

- ⅞ yard of coordinating solid fabric for tucked panel and backing
- ½ yard of print for flat panel
- Acrylic ruler with marked grid
- Removable fabric-marking pen, pencil, or chalk marker
- Matching all-purpose thread
- Size 80/12 sewing-machine needle
- Bamboo pointer & creaser
- Hand sewing needle

Basic Tucked Place Mats

Choose a bold print and a solid accent fabric for this basic place mat. A lightweight cotton or cotton/linen blend is perfect for the flat panel, and silk doupioni is a lovely choice for the tucks.

SHOPPING LIST

After you've brought home new fabric, it's easy to forget the care instructions. When you're at the store, write down the care details from the end of the bolt, along with a fabric description, in a small notebook or PDA. If you record the information on paper or a note card, add a 1" square of the fabric.

Instructions

1. From the print, cut two 13" squares. From the solid fabric, cut two 13" x 15" rectangles for the tucked panels.
2. With wrong sides together, fold a 13" x 15" panel in half widthwise, aligning the 13" edges; press. This is the folded edge of the center vertical tuck. Press three parallel foldlines on each side of the center fold, spacing them 1¾" apart.

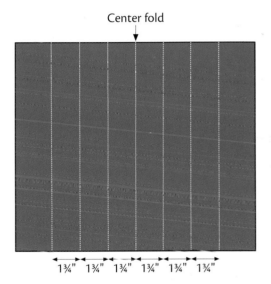

Center fold

1¾" 1¾" 1¾" 1¾" 1¾" 1¾"

SEW SMART

For fewer tucks, press just two parallel foldlines on each side of the center fold, 2" apart.

3. Set your sewing machine for a 2.5 mm- or 3.0 mm-long straight stitch. Insert a new size 80/12 machine needle (unless you're using a specialty fabric that requires a different-size needle).

4. Straight stitch ½" from each pressed foldline. Press the tucks to one side.

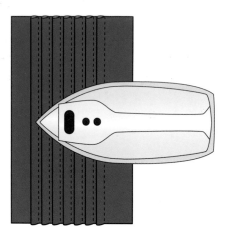

Tucks add texture and dimension.

5. Using the fabric marker, draw a horizontal line perpendicular to the tucks and centered between the upper and lower edges. Stitch on the marked line to secure the tucks.

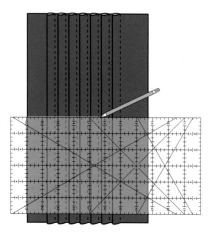

6. Press the upper and lower 3" of the tuck ends in the opposite direction. Draw another horizontal line 2½" from the upper and lower edges; stitch along each marked line to secure the tucks.

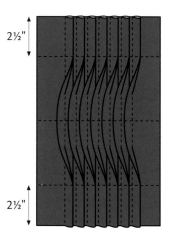

2½"

2½"

FLOWER POWER

When stitching horizontal lines on tucked panels, you don't have to use a straight stitch. Experiment with the built-in decorative stitches on your sewing machine to add a special touch.

Use matching thread for a subtle effect. Or use contrasting thread for more pop. Stitch each row using a different decorative stitch. The possibilities are endless.

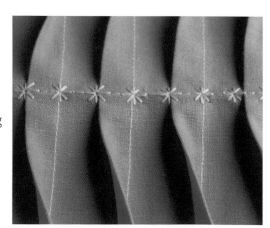

7. Trim the tucked panel to 7" wide, centering the tucks.
8. With right sides together, align the tucked panel and the print panel along the 13"-long edge; pin. Stitch using a ½" seam allowance to form the place-mat front.

9. Press the seam to set the stitches, and then press the seam allowances away from the tucks. Repeat to create the second place-mat front.
10. With right sides together, position the place-mat fronts on the backing fabric. Pin parallel to the place-mat edges, keeping the pins away from the edges to avoid nicking the scissor blades.

11. Cut out the place-mat backs using the fronts as patterns. After cutting, add a few more pins closer to the cut edges to hold the layers for sewing.
12. Using a ½" seam allowance, stitch around the place-mat perimeter, pivoting at the corners and leaving a 6" opening on the short edge without the tucks. Repeat to stitch the second place mat. Press the seams to set the stitches. Clip the corners to reduce the bulk.

6" opening

13. Turn each place mat right side out. Use a bamboo pointer & creaser to gently shape the corners from the inside. Press the outer edges, turning under the seam allowances at the opening. Slipstitch the opening closed.

Multicolored Tucked Place Mats

Select two solid fabrics for this place mat. High-contrast colors, such as black and white, set a dramatic mood, while subdued colors like the grayed blue and warm green in the featured place mats add sophistication to a scheme. Designate one color as fabric A and the other as fabric B.

COLOR WHEEL

When choosing fabrics for a place mat, look to the color wheel for inspiration. Complementary colors—purple and yellow, for example—are modern and bold. Colors closer to each other on the wheel, such as blue-green and blue-violet, are more soothing.

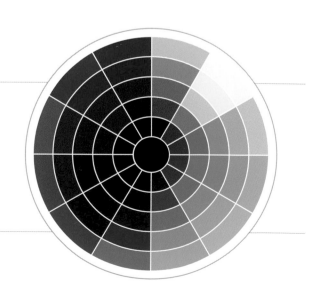

You'll Need

Yardages are based on 42"-wide fabric.
Materials listed will make two 12" x 18" place mats with alternating colors.

- ½ yard of fabric A for tucked panel
- ½ yard of fabric B for tucked panel
- ½ yard of fabric for backing
- Acrylic ruler with marked grid
- Removable fabric-marking pen, pencil, or chalk marker
- Matching all-purpose thread
- Size 80/12 sewing-machine needle
- Bamboo pointer & creaser
- Hand-sewing needle
- Sequins and beads

Instructions

1. From fabric A and fabric B *each*, cut six 2¼" x 13" strips for the tucks, two 2½" x 13" strips for the tucks and one 13" square for the flat panel.

2. Arrange the strips as shown below for one place mat.

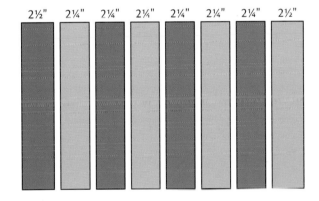

| 2½" | 2¼" | 2¼" | 2¼" | 2¼" | 2¼" | 2¼" | 2½" |

3. With right sides together and using a ¼" seam allowance, stitch the strips. Repeat to stitch the strips for the second place mat.

4. Press the seams flat to set the stitches, and then press the seam allowances open. With wrong sides together, fold the strips at the seamlines, encasing the seam allowances; press. (Each seamline will be the ridge of a stitched tuck.) Stitch ½" from each folded seamline to form a tuck.

5. Continue as instructed in steps 7–9 of "Basic Tucked Place Mats" on page 27.

6. Using the photo below as a guide, gently fold the tucks in alternating directions and secure with a combination of sequins and beads.

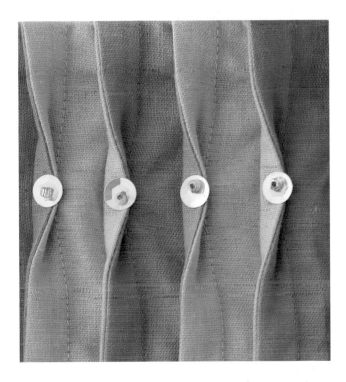

7. Continue as directed in steps 10–13 on page 27 to complete the place mats.

Tie TABLE RUNNER

Men's ties come in a wide array of colors and patterns. Who can resist using them in a variety of home-decorating projects? Twelve silk ties combine in this easy-sew table runner. Before you begin, launder or dry-clean the ties.

Designed by Kate Bashynski

You'll Need

Yardages are based on 42"-wide fabric. Materials listed make one 11"-wide runner; the length will depend on the number and width of the ties.

- Assortment of men's ties, eight or more
- ½ yard of muslin for foundation
- ½ yard of flannel for backing
- Seam ripper
- Acrylic ruler with marked grid
- Fabric marker
- Coordinating all-purpose thread
- Bamboo pointer & creaser
- Hand sewing needle

Instructions

1. Carefully inspect each tie for stains and wear, such as frayed edges or snags. Discard any ties that are too damaged. Sort the ties into compatible color combinations. The ties in the featured table runner have several common colors, but you may prefer a bolder combination, with every tie a different color palette.
2. Disassemble each tie, removing all the stitching, interfacing, and lining to yield the largest possible piece of fabric. Press out the folds.
3. Cut two 13"-long sections from the narrow end and midsection of each tie, not including the point at the end or the seam that often occurs in the middle area; reserve the wide ends for another project. (If you use the wider ends in this runner, you'll have fewer ties and less variety.) Cut just one section from each tie if you have many ties to choose from. You'll need approximately 14 to 16 strips, depending on the widths of the sections.

TIE TREASURE HUNT

Here are places to look for unwanted men's ties:

- Dig through your dad's, brother's, boyfriend's, husband's, grandfather's, or uncle's closet (ask permission first).
- Check local tag and yard sales.
- Visit second-hand, thrift, or consignment shops.
- Tell friends and coworkers you're collecting ties, and ask them to be on the lookout.

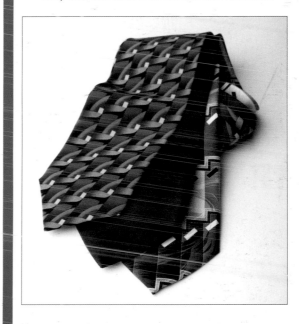

4. Cut off the selvages from the muslin and trim it to 12" wide.

5. Arrange the 13"-long strips on a flat surface, alternating wide and narrow ends.

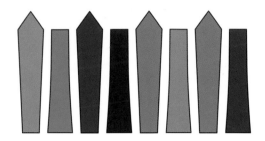

6. Place the muslin on your work surface. Position the first tie strip right side up on one end of the muslin; pin. Baste the strip in place.

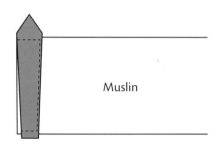

Muslin

7. With right sides together and raw edges aligned, place the second strip over the first strip; pin through all layers. Using the ruler and fabric marker, draw a line along the inside edges of the two strips. Stitch on the marked line; press to set the stitches.

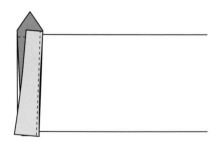

8. Flip over the second strip and press it away from the first. This is often referred to as the "sew and flip" method of piecing fabric strips. Repeat the process until the muslin base fabric is covered to the desired length.

9. Baste around the runner perimeter. Trim the tie ends even with the muslin base.

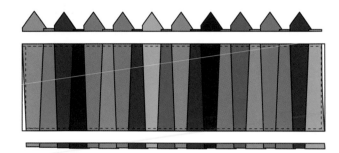

10. Cut the backing from the flannel fabric using the table-runner top as a pattern. With right sides together, pin the table-runner top and backing, securing all layers.

11. Using a ½" seam allowance, stitch around the perimeter, pivoting at the corners and leaving a 6" opening on one long edge for turning. Press the perimeter seams to set the stitches. Clip the corners to reduce the bulk. Or try a technique used to construct ties called "wrapped" corners, on the facing page.

12. Turn the table runner right side out through the opening. Use a bamboo pointer & creaser to gently shape each corner from the inside. Turn under the seam allowances at the opening and press; pin. Slipstitch the opening closed.

SILK SCARF

Use the same technique to create a scarf—just make a simple size adjustment.

♦ Start with a 6"- to 7"-wide strip of light-weight muslin or batiste for the base. Make the scarf as long as you wish, seaming two or more strips to make a longer base if necessary.

♦ Stitch tie strips to the base as directed for the table runner.

♦ Use a light rayon or silk charmeuse fabric for the backing.

♦ Hand stitch beads to the scarf ends to add a touch of sparkle.

WRAPPED CORNERS

Use this method to get very neat, crisp corners.

♦ With right sides together, stitch both table-runner long edges, leaving a 6" opening on one edge for turning. Press the seams flat to set the stitches.

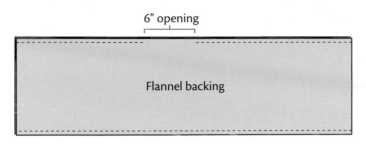

6" opening

Flannel backing

♦ At each corner, fold the seam allowances over the stitching toward the backing; pin. Stitch the short ends of the table runner, securing the folded seam allowances.

♦ Clip the corner seam allowances to reduce the bulk; press.

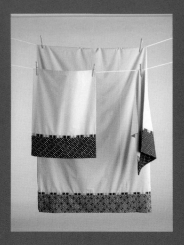

CUSTOM BED AND BATH

The bedroom and bath offer the ultimate retreat from a hectic, fast-paced world. Considering their multipurpose nature—rest and rejuvenation, the place where we begin and end each day—don't these rooms deserve our creative attention?

A quick bedroom makeover logically begins with the refurbishment of the largest component—the bed. Sheets trimmed in retro rickrack and a tailored bed skirt let you indulge your love of fabric. Tab curtains and a hanging lamp encircled in silk add color and pattern to any scheme. For the shower, an organizer made from two towels holds bath accessories neatly and safely. Go ahead, make your bed-and-bath oasis an expression of your personal style.

TRIM Time

Transform a ho-hum bedroom into a space with personality—it's fun, fabulous, and easy to do!
All it takes is rickrack, a bit of sewing time, and a little glue.

Designed by Pam Archer

You'll Need

Materials listed make a sheet set, consisting of two pillowcases and one top sheet, and one lampshade.

For sheet set:
- 1 flat sheet
- 2 standard pillowcases
- 2½ yards of medium Delft blue rickrack
- 5 yards *each* of baby Yale blue and jumbo green rickrack

For twin sheet:
- 2 yards of medium Delft blue rickrack
- 4 yards *each* of baby Yale blue and jumbo green rickrack

For full sheet:
- 2½ yards of medium Delft blue rickrack
- 5 yards *each* of baby Yale blue and jumbo green rickrack

For queen sheet:
- 2¾ yards of medium Delft blue rickrack
- 5½ yards *each* of baby Yale blue and jumbo green rickrack

For king sheet:
- 3¼ yards of medium Delft blue rickrack
- 6½ yards *each* of baby Yale blue and jumbo green rickrack
- Acrylic ruler with marked grid
- Air-soluble fabric marker
- Seam sealant
- Monofilament thread
- Bobbin thread to match sheet color
- Chopstick (optional)

For lampshade:
- White lampshade: 7" tall, 3½" upper diameter, 11" lower diameter
- 1⅛ yards of baby Yale blue rickrack
- 1 yard *each* of jumbo green and medium Delft blue rickrack
- Acrylic ruler with marked grid
- Air-soluble fabric marker
- Craft or fabric glue
- Seam sealant

Preparation

1. Preshrink the sheet, pillowcases, and trim. Because the fiber content may vary, the fabric and trim may shrink differently. Preshrinking prevents puckers after laundering the finished pieces.
2. Before washing the trim, add a dot of seam sealant to each end to prevent raveling; let dry. Place the trim in a lingerie bag so it doesn't tangle.
3. Press the laundered items to prevent bumpy sewing and puckers.
4. Before cutting the rickrack, apply a dot of seam sealant to the cutting line and let dry.

RETRO CHIC

Rickrack has been around for a long time. It was first noted on garment edges in the early 1800s. Original rickrack was hand crocheted. Now it's mass produced in a variety of sizes and colors, and its textures have expanded to include chenille rickrack.

Pillowcase Instructions

1. Cut the baby Yale blue and the jumbo green rickrack into four equal lengths *each*; cut the medium Delft blue rickrack in half.
2. Using a seam ripper and starting at the pillowcase opening, release one pillowcase side seam 5".
3. Working on the pillowcase right side, place one piece of baby Yale blue rickrack along the edge, aligning the points with the edge; pin. Stitch the rickrack down the center, using the monofilament thread in the top and thread to match the pillowcase in the bobbin.
4. Place another baby Yale blue rickrack piece over the hem topstitching; stitch.

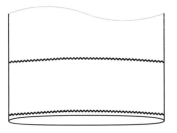

STITCHING TIPS

Using clear monofilament in the sewing machine needle allows errant stitches to blend in. Here are a few more rickrack tips:

♦ Stitch down the center of the rickrack. On jumbo rickrack, you can also stitch across the upper and lower points if desired. Stitching the points eliminates the need to press them after laundering.
♦ Use a chopstick to keep rickrack points in the proper position while sewing.
♦ Avoid pulling rickrack when measuring, pinning, or stitching—rickrack will stretch. Its flexibility is a great feature when adding it to curves or a lampshade. However, for straight-line applications, lay the rickrack flat and let it relax before sewing to prevent puckers.

5. With the acrylic ruler and air-soluble marker, draw parallel placement lines 1", 2", and 3" from the edge.

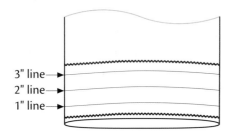

3" line→
2" line→
1" line→

SEW SMART

Most pillowcase hem and sheet headers measure 4". If your linen hems vary, space the Delft blue and green rickrack rows evenly between the two rows of Yale blue rickrack.

6. Pin the medium Delft blue rickrack length along the 2" line. Stitch down the rickrack center.

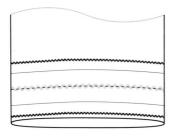

7. Pin the jumbo green rickrack lengths along the 1" and 3" lines. Stitch down the rickrack centers and, if desired, across the upper and lower points.

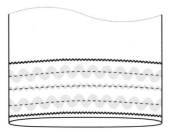

8. Trim the rickrack ends flush with the pillowcase raw edges. With right sides together and matching the rickrack trim, repin the pillowcase side seam. Stitch the seam and zigzag or serge-finish the raw edges.

Sheet Instructions

1. To add trim to the sheet header, cut the rickrack yardage into two equal pieces of baby Yale blue rickrack and two equal pieces of jumbo green rickrack. (There's no need to cut the medium Delft blue rickrack because you'll stitch just one piece.) Before cutting the rickrack, add a dot of seam sealant to the cutting line and let dry.

2. Release 5" of each side hem at the top of the sheet.

3. With the sheet right side up, place one baby Yale blue rickrack length along the sheet upper edge, aligning the points with the edge; stitch.

4. Place another baby Yale blue rickrack length along the header topstitching; stitch.

5. With the acrylic ruler and air-soluble marker, draw parallel lines 1", 2", and 3" from the header edge. Pin the medium Delft blue rickrack along the 2" line; stitch.

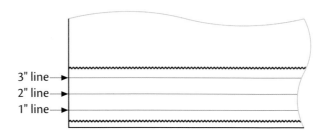

3" line→
2" line→
1" line→

6. Pin the jumbo green rickrack along the 1" and 3" lines; stitch down the center and, if desired, across the upper and lower points.

7. Refold the sheet side hems and stitch with matching thread.

4. With the acrylic ruler and air-soluble marker, mark two parallel lines 1" and 2" from the lampshade lower edge.

5. Working in 6"-long segments, apply a thin bead of glue along the 1" line. Finger-press the jumbo green rickrack in place, finishing the ends as for the baby rickrack. Apply the medium Delft blue rickrack along the 2" line. Set the lampshade aside and allow the glue to dry.

RICKRACK WON'T DO?

Consider using different trims to embellish your sheets. It's the same concept—you'll just get a different look.

♦ Stitch on washable grosgrain ribbon in solids, stripes, or plaids for a beautiful effect.

♦ Layer ribbons for a fancier effect. Layering adds dimension and texture and breaks up the color of a single ribbon. Simply place a narrower ribbon on a wider ribbon and stitch together. Try alternating rows of patterned and solid ribbon.

♦ Substitute bias tape, gimp, and soutache for creative alternatives to ribbon and rickrack.

♦ Use up your trim stash. There's no rule that says the trim must go across the entire sheet width. Consider staggering a variety of ribbons and leaving their ends loose. (Be sure to add seam sealant to the cut ends, or tie a knot in each end.)

♦ Prevent visual overload by limiting your color palette to three colors and using no more than five different trims. Keeping the embellishment simple results in a light accent and prevents the header from puckering due to additional stitching lines.

Lampshade Instructions

1. Beginning ¼" to the left of the lampshade seam and close to the lower edge, apply a thin, 6"-long bead of glue.

2. Place the baby Yale blue rickrack over the glue, keeping one edge of the rickrack points even with the lampshade edge; finger-press evenly. Apply another 6"-long bead of glue and finger-press the rickrack. Repeat until the rickrack meets at the lampshade seam.

3. Overlap the rickrack slightly, add a drop of seam sealant, and cut it to meet at the seam; glue.

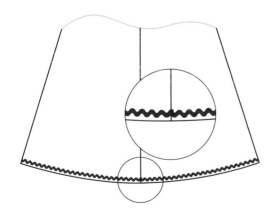

Designer SHEET and PILLOWCASES

Embellish new sheets with eye-catching print coordinates, or revive an existing set to make it look like new. Reintroduce the same fabrics in pillows, quilts, or window treatments for boutique appeal.

Designed by Lisa Shepard Stewart

You'll Need
Yardages are based on 42"-wide fabric.

- 1 flat sheet
- 2 standard pillowcases
- Nondirectional print (see "Home-Sewing Glossary" on page 95) for sheet hem:
    - 2 yards for twin sheet
    - 2⅝ yards for full sheet
    - 2⅞ yards for queen sheet
    - 3¼ yards for king sheet
- 1⅓ yards of nondirectional print for pillowcase hems
- Coordinating print for flat-piping trim on pillowcases and sheet:
    - ½ yard for twin or full sheet
    - ⅝ yard for full, queen, or king sheet

Preparation
Because the sheets will be laundered frequently, choose machine-washable fabrics and prewash them at least once. Test for colorfastness, especially if the sheet fabric is a light color. The same pretreatment should be given to any trims.

Sheet Instructions
1. Cut off the top hem from the sheet, including any piping.
2. Measure the sheet width. From the lengthwise grain of the main fabric, cut a strip 14" wide and equal in length to the sheet width plus 1". Press under ½" on one long edge of the strip.
3. From the width of the coordinating print for the flat piping, cut as many 3"-wide strips as needed to make a strip equal to the main-fabric strip. Stitch the strips together end to end to make one long strip; press the seam allowances open. Trim the strip to the length of the main-fabric strip.

4. Fold the flat-piping strip in half lengthwise with wrong sides together; press. With the wrong side of the sheet facing up, pin the flat piping to the sheet raw edge, extending the piping raw edges ¼" above the sheet raw edge, and the ends ½" on each side edge; baste.

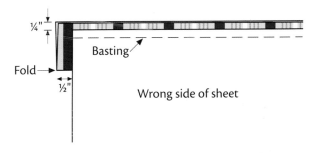

Wrong side of sheet

5. Turn the sheet to the right side. With right sides together, pin the long, unpressed edge of the main-fabric strip over the flat piping, aligning the main-fabric long raw edge with the sheet raw edge and extending the ends ½" on each side edge. Stitch through all layers using a ½" seam allowance; press the seam to set the stitches.

Wrong side of main fabric

Sheet placement
(hidden under main fabric)

6. Fold the main-fabric strip lengthwise with right sides together, aligning the main-fabric pressed edge and the flat-piping pressed edge. Stitch each end using a ½" seam allowance. Trim the corners to reduce the bulk; turn and press. Topstitch the main-fabric folded edge close to the piping folded edge; press.

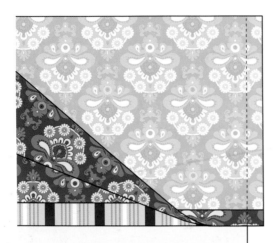

Right side of sheet

Pillowcase Instructions

1. Cut off the hem from each pillowcase, including any piping.
2. Measure the pillowcase circumference and add 1". From the flat-piping fabric, cut two 3"-wide strips. Stitch the strips together end to end to make one long strip; press the seam allowances open. Cut the strip to equal the pillowcase circumference plus 1".
3. With right sides together, fold the strip in half widthwise. Sew the ends with a ½" seam allowance to form a tube; press the seam allowances open. Fold the tube in half lengthwise with wrong sides together; press. Pin the flat-piping tube to the pillowcase right side, extending the flat-piping raw edges ¼" beyond the pillowcase edge and aligning the seams; baste.
4. From the main fabric, cut a 16"-wide strip equal in length to the pillowcase circumference plus 1". With right sides together, fold the strip in half widthwise. Sew the ends together with a ½" seam allowance to form a tube; press the seam allowances open. Turn under and press ½" on one long edge of the fabric tube. Fold the tube in half lengthwise with wrong sides together, extending the unpressed edge ½" beyond the pressed edge.
5. With right sides together, pin the long unpressed edge of the tube over the piping, aligning the main fabric raw edge with the pillowcase raw edge. Stitch using a ½" seam allowance; press the seam to set the stitches. To form a self-lining, turn the pressed fabric edge to the pillowcase wrong side, encasing the seam allowances; pin. Topstitch the main-fabric folded edge close to the flat-piping folded edge; press.
6. Repeat to add a border to the second pillowcase.

SKIRTING the Issue

A daybed with a trundle bed below is great for children's sleepovers or guests, but it's less than desirable to look at. Adding a typical bed skirt to camouflage the lower mattress can create a few problems—the bed skirt is likely to get caught in the lifting mechanism of the trundle bed and shift out of place. A custom bed skirt created in individual sections and attached by Velcro tape is a smart solution.

Designed by Cindy Kacynski

You'll Need

Yardages are based on 54"-wide solid-colored fabric or nondirectional print (see "Home-Sewing Glossary" on page 95).

Materials listed make one twin-size bed skirt with box pleats. For a plain skirt, see "Simplify It" on page 45.

- ♦ 4¼ yards of fabric for skirt
- ♦ 6½ yards of ¾"-wide Velcro
- ♦ Matching all-purpose thread
- ♦ Industrial glue

Instructions for Bed Skirt with Box Pleats

1. Measure the bed length and add 19" for the front and back panels. Measure the bed width and add 3" for the end panels. Measure the bed-frame depth (from the bed-frame upper edge to the floor) and add 2¼".

2. Using each total measurement from the previous step, cut two rectangles equal to the front- and back-panel length, by the bed-frame depth. Cut two rectangles equal to the end-panel width, by the bed-frame depth. On each rectangle, designate one edge as the lower edge.

3. Double fold all rectangle lower edges ¾" to the wrong side; press. Stitch close to the first fold on each rectangle to form the lower hem. Repeat for all rectangle short edges.

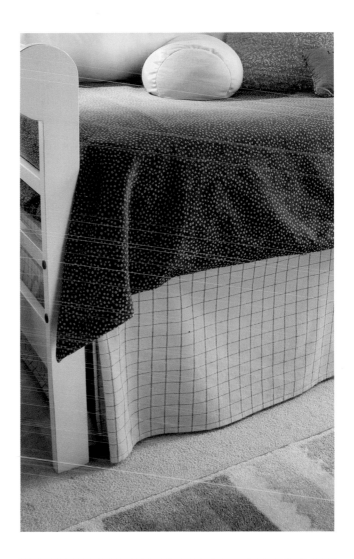

SEW SMART

Home-decorating cotton fabric works well for this project. Its "hand"—the weight and feel of the fabric—keeps the pleats crisp and the panels smooth.

4. Zigzag or serge-finish the upper edge of each rectangle. Fold ¾" to the wrong side once; press.

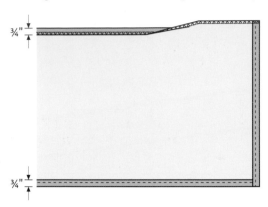

5. Create a 2"-wide single pleat at the end of each long rectangle; pin. Create a box pleat at the midpoint of each long rectangle as shown; pin.

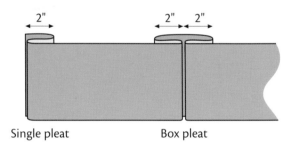

Single pleat   Box pleat

6. Measure the upper edge of each pleated panel and compare it to the bed-frame length. If necessary, adjust the pleats; baste the pleats at the upper edge through all layers.

7. Cut a piece of Velcro to fit the upper edge of each rectangle. Pin the hook side to each upper-edge fold; stitch both long tape edges to secure. Remove the basting.

8. Glue the loop section of the tape to the bed-frame upper edge. Let dry, following the manufacturer's instructions.

9. Attach the bed-skirt sections to the frame. Remove the sections as needed to access a trundle bed or to launder the skirt.

Velcro lets you easily remove the bed skirt.

Design Options

For a different look—gathered or tailored—try one of these variations for a trundle-bed skirt. You can also make a bed skirt for a conventional bed. Never again will your bed skirt shift underneath your mattress, and you won't wrestle with your mattress to remove the bed skirt for washing.

Gather It

Cut the bed-skirt sections twice the bed length and width, by the bed-frame depth, plus 3". Sew a rolled-edge hem along the lower edge and each short edge of each rectangle. Double fold each upper edge ¾" to the wrong side. Sew two rows of gathering stitches. Pull the bobbin threads evenly to gather the upper edge to the bed-frame length or width, depending on the panel. Stitch the hook portion of the Velcro to the wrong side of the gathered edge. Glue the loop section of the tape to the bed-frame upper edge.

Simplify It

To make a plain skirt for a trundle bed, you'll need approximately 3¾ yards of fabric and Velcro. Follow the measuring instructions in step 1, page 43, adding only 3" to the bed-length measurement rather than 19". Skip steps 5 and 6.

Glue It

For a conventional bed with a box spring, measure the bed depth from the top of the box spring and add 1". Glue the loop side of the hook-and-loop tape to the box spring.

TRY THIS!

Make a bed skirt to camouflage other areas in your home. For example, add a skirt to a bathroom vanity to create a hidden storage space. Put a skirt on a set of shelves to add color and hide junk. You can also add embellishments, such as embroidery, trim, crystals, and more.

Another option is a gathered skirt, which has more fullness than one made with box pleats.

ROOM with a VIEW

Give any room a quick and inexpensive makeover with simple tab-top curtains. To create the two-tone look on the tabs and tiebacks, use the *wrong side* of the main fabric for the contrast strips.

Designed by Sandra Geiger

You'll Need

Yardages are based on 54"-wide fabric. Materials listed make one set of 46" x 55" tab curtains and two tiebacks.

- 4¾ yards of drapery-weight fabric (Purchase extra fabric to match a pattern repeat; see "Matching a Pattern Repeat" on page 92.)
- ½ yard of contrast fabric (only needed if your drapery fabric won't work as the contrast)
- 3½ yards of lining fabric
- ¾ yard of heavyweight sew-in interfacing
- Rotary cutter, ruler, and mat
- Matching all-purpose thread
- Seam roll
- Hand-sewing needle
- Four ½"-diameter plastic rings
- 2 small cup hooks

Fabric Guidelines

- Select a drapery-weight fabric that has a stable weave. Slippery or unstable fabrics are more difficult to sew and can stretch over time.
- Lining provides energy-saving insulation and protects the curtain fabric from sun damage. Lining also maintains a uniform look from the exterior of the home.

Cutting

Trim the selvages from the drapery fabric and lining.

From the drapery-weight fabric, cut:
- 2 curtain panels, the fabric width x 64"
- 20 tab pieces, 3½" x 10" (if using wrong side of same fabric for two-tone look)*
- 4 tieback pieces, 3½" x 24" (if using wrong side of same fabric for two-tone look)*
- 2 facings, the fabric width x 5½"

* If using a separate contrast fabric (below), you'll need to cut only 10 tab pieces and 2 tieback pieces from your main fabric.

From the contrast fabric (if using), cut:
- 10 tab pieces, 3½" x 10"
- 2 tieback pieces, 3½" x 24"

From the lining fabric, cut:
- 2 panels, the fabric width x 56"

From the interfacing, cut:
- 2 pieces, 6½" x 24"

DIFFERENT DIMENSIONS

The featured curtains are designed for a 50"- to 51"-high window. To create curtains for a window of a different height, follow these guidelines:
- Drapery-weight fabric: Cut two rectangles the fabric width x the window height plus 9".
- Lining fabric: Cut two rectangles 6" narrower and 8" shorter than the curtain panel.
- For less fullness, cut each curtain panel narrower than the full fabric width; cut the lining accordingly.

Curtain Instructions

Use ½" seam allowances unless otherwise noted.

1. Pair two tab strips with contrasting sides together; stitch both long edges. Press the seam allowances open over the seam roll to prevent creases. Turn the tab right side out, and then press it flat, centering the seams to create a two-tone effect. Repeat to stitch the remaining tabs.

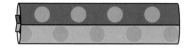

2. Position one curtain panel wrong side up on a flat work surface. Designate one short edge as the upper edge.

3. Trim one lining panel 6" narrower than the curtain panel.

4. Center the lining panel right side up over the curtain panel so that 3" of the drapery fabric shows on each edge. Align the upper edges; pin. Mark the curtain side edges 8" above the lower edge.

5. Fold the curtain side edges 1½" toward the wrong side, beginning at the upper edge and ending at the 8" mark; press. Fold again 1½", enclosing the lining edges; press and pin. Stitch close to the first folds.

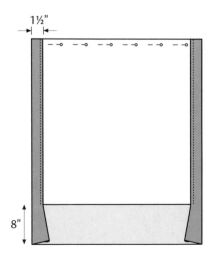

6. Below the 8" mark, fold the side edges toward the wrong side at a 30° angle; press.

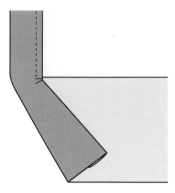

7. Position the curtain right side up on the flat work surface. Fold each tab in half widthwise. Pin a tab at each curtain side edge, with the raw edges aligned and the folded ends *down*. Space the remaining three tabs evenly along the upper edge; baste.

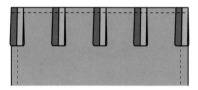

8. Designate one long edge of the facing as the upper edge. Fold the lower edge 1" toward the wrong side; press.

9. With right sides together, center the facing over the curtain, aligning the upper edges and sandwiching the tabs. Stitch the upper edge through all layers using a 1" seam allowance.

10. Fold the facing to the curtain wrong side; press. Trim the facing ends to 1" and turn them to the inside, aligning the folds with the curtain edges. Edgestitch the facing side and lower edges.

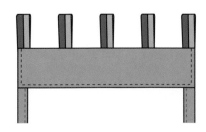

11. Fold the curtain lower edge 4" toward the wrong side; press. Fold again 4" toward the wrong side, forming a mitered corner; press and pin. Stitch close to the first fold. Repeat steps 2–11 to construct the second curtain.

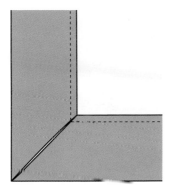

Tieback Instructions

1. Pair two tieback strips with contrasting right sides together; pin and stitch along one long edge. Press the seam allowances open. Position one interfacing rectangle over the tieback wrong side. Baste around the perimeter ¼" from the edges.

2. Fold the tieback in half lengthwise with right sides together, pin. Stitch the long edge; press the seam allowances open over a seam roll to prevent creases.

3. Turn the tieback right side out, and then press it flat, centering the seams for a two-tone effect. At each end, turn the raw edges in ½"; pin. Slipstitch the ends closed.

4. Designate one long edge as the tieback upper edge. Hand stitch a plastic ring at each upper corner. Repeat steps 1–4 to construct the second tieback.

5. After hanging the curtains, determine the wall placement for the tieback cup hooks. Install the hooks according to the manufacturer's instructions. Wrap the tiebacks around the curtains and secure the rings on the cup hooks.

SUIT YOUR STYLE

To customize your curtains, look for tieback rings and cup hooks in various sizes and metallic finishes. You'll find them at home-improvement or hardware stores, or even in department stores with home-decorating departments.

Bathroom ORGANIZER

Keep soap, shampoo, lotion, and bath salts handy by hanging this organizer on the same rings as your shower curtain. The project sews up quickly using two matching hand towels.

Designed by Marla Stefanelli

Instructions

1. Look at the towels and consider any decorative bands before beginning. This project used towels with a decorative band across one end, which was placed to be visible when the lower pocket was folded up and stitched. If your towels have a band at each end, you don't have to worry about the placement.

2. Remove the tags and preshrink the towels. To determine the wrong side of each towel, look at the hem at one short end. The hem is usually turned and stitched to the wrong side.

SEW SMART

The towels may be slightly distorted after prewashing. Take this into account when measuring and cutting the pocket pieces. Where edges are supposed to align, ease in the extra fullness or stretch the width so the edges match.

3. To create two pockets from one towel, cut off 6½" from the end with the decorative band, and cut off 4½" from the opposite end. Set aside the leftover center section to test install the grommets.

4. On the remaining towel, turn the short end without the decorative band 2" to the wrong side and stitch next to the hem to secure the layers.

SEW SMART

When stitching over several bulky fabric layers, sew slowly to avoid breaking the machine needle.

5. Place the towel wrong side up on a flat surface with the turned edge at the top. Measure 12½" from the lower edge and place several pins across the towel to mark the line. Measure 18½" from the lower edge and place several more pins across the towel to mark this line.

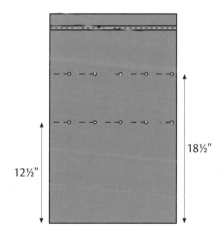

6. With the wrong side up, position the 4½"-wide pocket strip across the towel, aligning the raw edge of the strip with the upper row of pins. Pin the pocket, and then remove the pins marking the row. Stitch ½" from the raw edge to secure the strip to the towel.

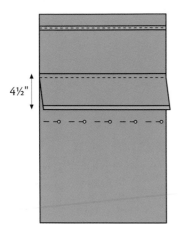

4½"

7. Fold the pocket strip up along the seam and pin at each side edge. With the wrong side up, position the 6½"-wide strip even with the remaining row of pins and stitch to the towel in the same manner. Fold up and pin the strip at each side edge.

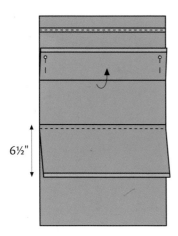

6½"

8. Fold the lower edge of the towel up 6" to form the lower pocket; pin at each side edge. Keeping the edges aligned, stitch down each side of the towel ¼" from the edge to secure the pockets. To form

the individual pockets, pin-mark a vertical line 5⅜" from each side edge. Stitch, backstitching at each upper edge of each row of pockets.

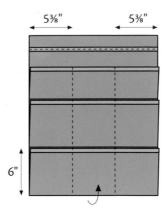

5⅜"   5⅜"

6"

9. Mark the grommet locations in the 2" section at the upper edge. The grommets should align with the shower curtain holes; most shower curtain holes are 6" apart, measuring from the hole centers. Find the vertical center of the organizer and mark a dot ¾" from the upper edge. Mark the placement for the remaining two grommets 6" on either side of the center grommet, also ¾" from the upper edge. See "Installing Grommets" on the facing page to complete the organizer.

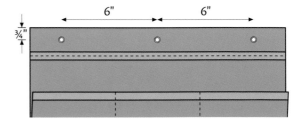

6"   6"

¾"

10. To hang the organizer, thread the rings that hold the shower curtain through the grommet holes.

INSTALLING GROMMETS

If you've never worked with grommets before, be sure to purchase a package that includes the setting tool.

Grommets consist of two pieces. The larger piece has a deeper center shank that goes through the fabric. This piece is inserted from the project right side. The remaining flatter ring is placed over the center shank on the wrong side. Then the setting tool is placed in the center shank from the wrong side and hit firmly with a hammer to "marry" the pieces.

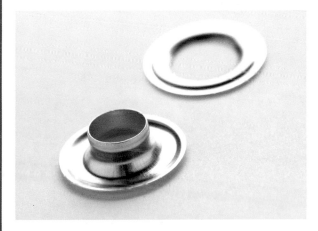

Always test install a grommet on the same thickness of fabric layers as the finished project. This will help determine if there is enough or too much fabric for the length of the shank, and how hard to hit the setting tool. If the installed grommet is loose, there probably isn't enough fabric to support it (not the case for this project). Add another fabric layer or apply interfacing to the fabric wrong side.

♦ To mark the grommet locations, use a craft knife or embroidery scissors to cut a small hole at each mark equal to the grommet measurement (⅜" in this project).

♦ Place the larger grommet piece through the hole from the right side. Turn the work over and place it over a scrap piece of 2" x 4" lumber. Place the lumber on a flat surface—a hard floor works best.

♦ Position the flat grommet ring over the shank with the rounded side facing up. Position the setting tool in the shank and hit firmly with a hammer. Don't hit too hard or you'll flatten and distort the grommet.

♦ If the grommet pieces won't join properly, there's probably too much fabric. Trim the hole a little larger or bevel the edges on thick fabrics.

SEW SMART
To hang the organizer from a small rod, omit the grommets and slide the rod through the rod pocket formed at the top.

Embellished LAMPSHADE

Create a dreamy addition to your decor with a simple lampshade makeover. Select a fabric with medium- to large-scale motifs, and then add dimension with buttons and hand stitching. Use matching yardage to create coordinating throw pillows and curtains.

Designed by Beth Bradley

You'll Need
- Lampshade
- ¼ to ½ yard of printed fabric, depending on the lampshade and the scale of the motifs
- Spray fabric adhesive
- Hand-embroidery needle
- Coordinating embroidery floss
- Assorted buttons
- Sharp scissors

Instructions
1. Select the fabric motifs you like best. Carefully cut around each motif; see "Make a Fuss" at right.
2. Arrange the motifs on the lampshade until you're happy with their placement. Spray adhesive on the wrong side of each motif. Position the motifs on the lampshade and finger-press to adhere them to the surface.
3. To add decorative hand stitching, thread the needle with three strands of embroidery floss. Knot the floss ends. Poke the needle through from inside the lampshade and stitch around the motifs' outer edges using one or more embroidery stitches. See "Hand Embroidery" on page 93.

4. Position the buttons as desired on the lampshade. Hand stitch them in place, knotting the thread ends on the inside.

MAKE A FUSS
To "fussy cut" means to select and cut out a particular area of printed fabric, rather than randomly cutting yardage. Quilters often use fussy cutting to achieve optimum design harmony in their quilts. It's also a great way to utilize small pieces of a favorite printed fabric. For the embellished lampshade, cut around the fabric motifs as roughly or as "fussily" as you please. Here are a few other fussy-cutting ideas:
- Cut out fun designs from printed oilcloth to make easy magnets.
- Select pretty floral designs to decorate a plain skirt or cardigan.
- Cut out a festive fabric motif to stitch onto a handmade greeting card.

LAMP of Luxury

Fashionable and functional, these works of art add romantic illumination to any room. Make several single lamps and cluster them outside for a perfect party accessory or hang them inside over a buffet.

Designed by Ellen March

You'll Need
Materials listed make one lamp.

- 1 yard of silk doupioni
- 1 yard of wide Jacquard ribbon
- Matching all-purpose thread
- 22-gauge copper wire
- Two 10"-diameter wire lamp rings
- Electrical tape
- One 1½" open S hook
- Wire cutter
- Pliers
- Seam sealant (optional)
- Lamp kit or string of white lights

Instructions

1. Using the copper wire and wire cutter, make a crossbar for one of the lamp rings. Curl the wire ends around the ring with pliers. Conceal the cut wire ends with electrical tape.

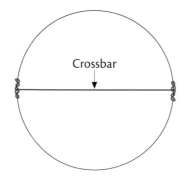

Crossbar

2. Attach the S hook at the crossbar center with a 6" length of copper wire; secure the S hook to the crossbar by wrapping each wire end around either side of the crossbar several times.

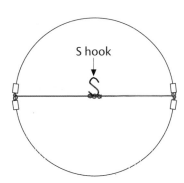

S hook

3. From the silk doupioni, cut a 14" x 32½" rectangle. (To create different-sized lanterns, vary the 14" measurement.)

SEW SMART

If your fabric is lightweight or sheer, use a French seam to conceal the raw edges on both sides of the finished piece. You'll need to cut your rectangle with a wider seam allowance on the 14" edge; see "Sewing a French Seam" on page 92.

4. Double fold the upper and lower raw edges of the silk rectangle ½" to the wrong side and press using your iron's silk setting, creating foldlines. Unfold the upper and lower folds.

5. On the fabric right side, pin the length of ribbon ¼" inside the second foldline at the lower edge. Topstitch with matching thread. Trim the ribbon ends.

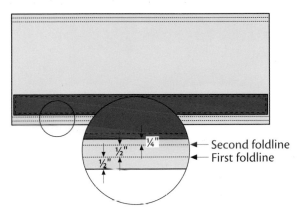

Second foldline
First foldline

6. Fold the fabric in half widthwise, with right sides together. Stitch the short raw edges together with a ½" seam allowance; press the seam allowances open. Turn the fabric right side out and refold the upper and lower folds.

7. Slide the lamp ring with crossbar inside the upper fold. Hand baste the folded edge to encase the lamp ring. At the wire, clip the fabric up to, but not touching, the second foldline. Apply seam sealant to the cut edges, if desired, and let dry.

8. Whipstitch the upper fold in place from the wrong side, encasing the lamp ring. Repeat, basting and stitching the lower fold to encase the remaining lamp ring, omitting the clips at the fold.

9. Insert a purchased lamp kit or light string into the frame. Use the S hook to anchor the light.

Lounge SACK

Stitch a simple beanbag chair to add extra seating in a dorm room or bedroom. A muslin lining keeps the stuffing in place and allows you to remove the chair cover for laundering.

Designed by Gena Bloemendaal

You'll Need

Yardages are based on 42"-wide fabric.

- 4½ yards of mediumweight fabric for outer cover
- 4½ yards of muslin for inner cover
- 22"-long zipper to blend with outer fabric
- 22"-long zipper to blend with muslin
- Matching all-purpose thread
- Polysterene beanbag beads (approximately 9 cubic feet) or shredded polyurethane foam filler (approximately 12 cubic feet)

Cutting

Enlarge the top-, bottom-, and side-panel pattern pieces on pages 61–63 as indicated to make full-size patterns.

From both the mediumweight fabric and the muslin, cut:

- 1 beanbag top
- 2 beanbag bottoms
- 4 beanbag side panels
- 2 rectangles, 2" x 3"

Instructions

Use ½" seam allowances unless otherwise noted.

1. Begin by installing the zipper on the muslin sack. Fold under ½" of one short side on each small muslin rectangle to make a zipper tab; press. Position each tab, folded edge down, at either end of the zipper. Stitch close to the folds to secure and stabilize the zipper ends.

2. Fold the straight edge on each muslin bottom piece under ½"; press. Position one folded edge over one side of the zipper close to the zipper teeth; stitch the edge, including the muslin tab at each end.

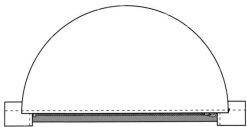

3. Repeat to attach the remaining bottom piece to the opposite zipper side. Open the zipper halfway; trim the tabs and any excess zipper tape even with the circle edge.

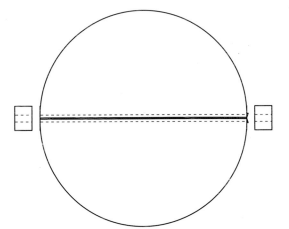

4. Baste the top and bottom circle perimeters ⅜" from the edge.

5. With right sides together, stitch two muslin side panels along one long edge. Repeat to stitch the remaining two panels. Open both sets of panels and place them right sides together. Stitch one side seam.

6. Open the panels and press the seam allowances to one side. Topstitch ¼" from each seamline, catching the seam allowances on the wrong side for strength.

7. With right sides together, stitch the remaining side seam so the panels form a tube. Press the final seam allowances to one side; topstitch.

HANDY HOLDER

Add a pocket to the beanbag cover to hold remotes, a journal, or an MP3 player.

8. Baste each tube upper and lower edge using a ⅜" seam allowance. Turn the cover wrong side out.

9. Fold the beanbag top in two directions and crease the fold at the edges. With right sides together and the creases aligned with the beanbag tube seams, pin the top to the smaller opening, aligning the basting. Pull the bobbin thread on the tube to slightly gather the opening. Repeat to pin the beanbag bottom to the larger opening.

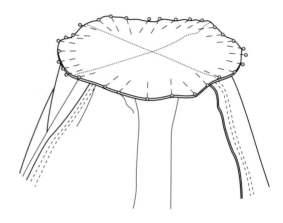

10. Stitch the top and bottom pieces to the tube, removing the pins as you sew. Stitch twice for strength.

11. Turn the finished muslin beanbag cover right side out through the zipper opening. Repeat steps 1–11 to stitch the beanbag outer cover.

12. Insert the muslin lining into the outer cover. Fill the muslin lining with stuffing; zip it shut. Zip the outer cover shut.

Beanbag Top
Enlarge pattern 125%.

Cut 1 from mediumweight fabric and 1 from muslin.

½" seam allowance

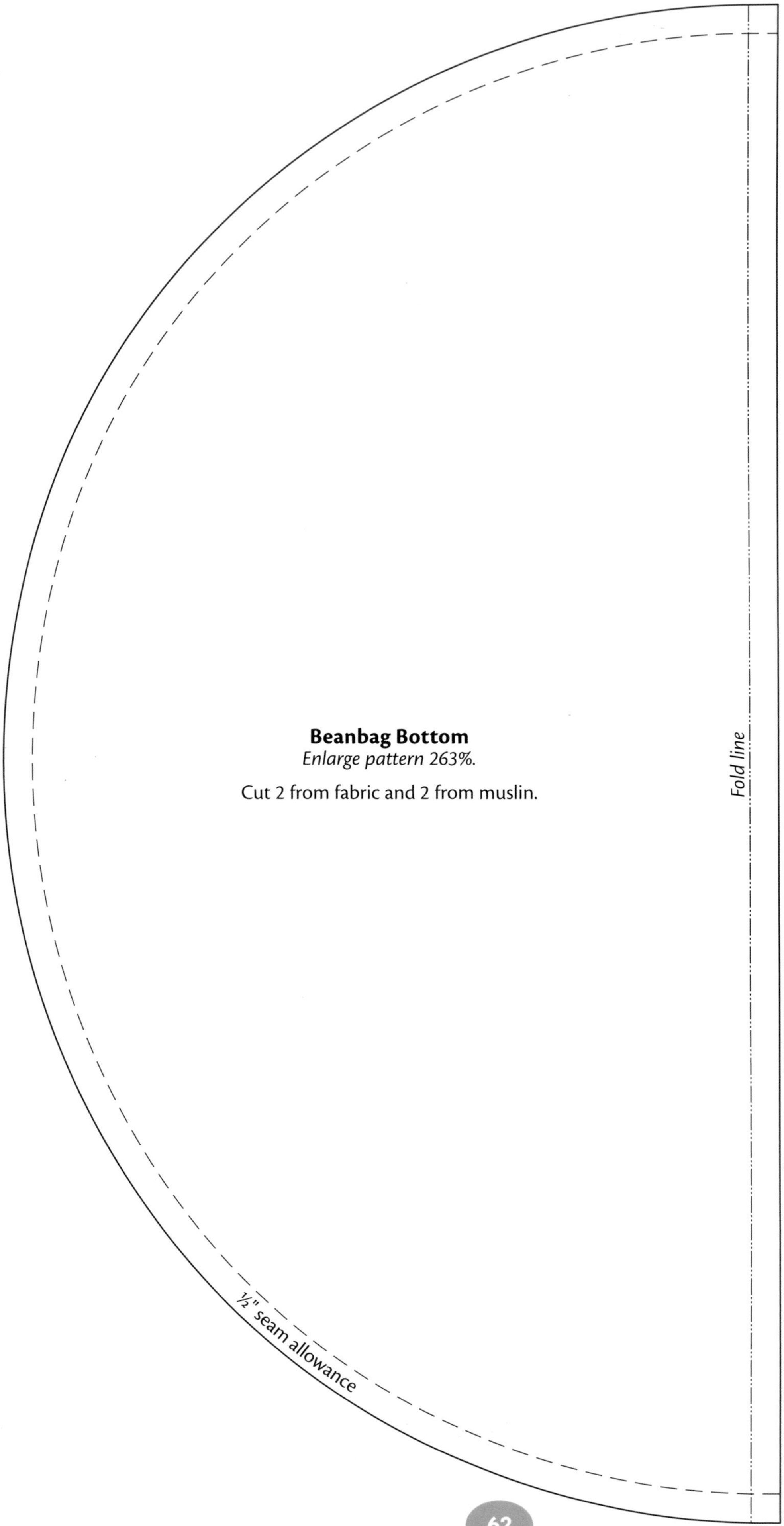

Beanbag Bottom
Enlarge pattern 263%.

Cut 2 from fabric and 2 from muslin.

Fold line

½" seam allowance

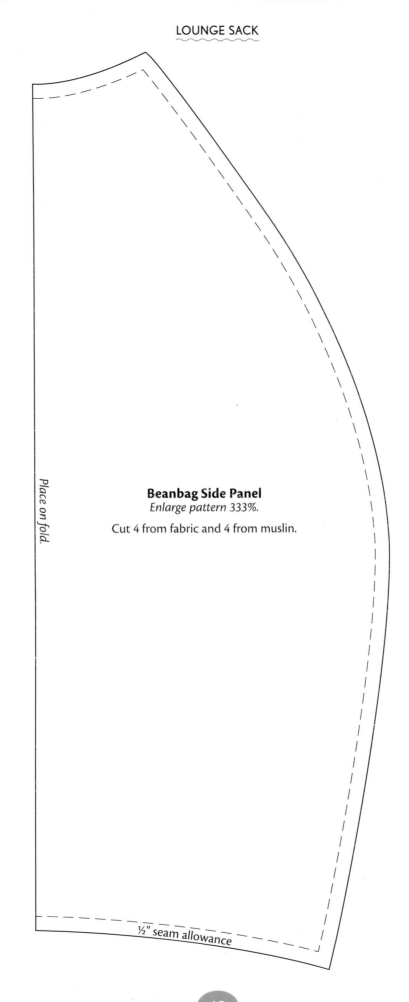

Place on fold.

Beanbag Side Panel
Enlarge pattern 333%.

Cut 4 from fabric and 4 from muslin.

½" seam allowance

PILLOW POWER

If you're new to sewing, a pillow is the perfect project. Pillows often provide the finishing touch in a decorating scheme, yet they require few materials or special tools. And a fabric that's too expensive for a large project suddenly looks affordable when calculating yardage for a pillow. Best of all, they stitch up in a flash.

Making a pillow is also a personal experience. You choose the shape, from a simple square or circle to an eye-catching cube. You select the fabrics, from shimmering silk to practical cotton. So get busy and stitch an array of pillows to complete your room—in your style.

EASTERN Influence

Beautiful silk fabric brings to mind traditional Eastern dress. Make a simple kimono-inspired silk obi to wrap a pillow for a chic touch.

Designed by Shannon Okey

You'll Need

Yardages are based on 42"-wide fabric.
Materials listed make one 12" x 15" pillow.

- ♦ ½ yard of silk fabric for pillow cover
- ♦ ⅜ yard of coordinating silk fabric for obi
- ♦ Matching all-purpose thread
- ♦ 2 decorative ½"-diameter buttons
- ♦ Tube turner for tie
- ♦ 12" x 15" rectangular pillow form

Instructions

Use ½" seam allowances unless otherwise noted.

1. From the pillow-cover fabric, cut two 13" x 16" rectangles and one 1½" x 22" strip (for the tie).

SAVE YOURSELF TIME

Instead of making the tie, save time by using ready-made coordinating silk ribbon or cording to secure the obi around the pillow.

2. Pin the two rectangles right sides together. Beginning on one long edge, stitch around the perimeter, pivoting at the corners and leaving a 7" opening for turning. Clip the corners to reduce the bulk.

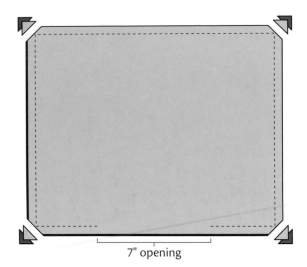

7" opening

3. Turn the pillow cover right side out, turning under the seam allowances at the opening. Press using your iron's silk setting. Insert the pillow form. Slipstitch the opening closed.
4. From the obi fabric, cut one rectangle 11" x 27". Fold the long edges 1½" toward the wrong side; press and pin. Fold the short edges 1½" toward the wrong side; press and pin.
5. Topstitch around the obi perimeter using a ⅜" seam allowance.

1½"

1½"

6. Center one button along one obi short edge on the fabric right side. Hand stitch the button in place. Repeat on the opposite obi short edge.
7. To create the tie, fold the 1½"-wide fabric strip in half lengthwise with right sides together; press. Stitch the long open edge using a ¼" seam allowance.
8. Trim the seam allowances. Use a tube turner to turn the strip right side out; press. Finish each end with a knot.
9. Wrap the obi around the pillow, aligning the buttons and short edges. Wind the tie around the buttons to secure the obi, tying a bow or knot as desired.

QUICK SWITCH

For more decor choices, make the obi reversible.
1. Cut one rectangle 9" x 25" *each* from two different fabrics.
2. Pin the rectangles with right sides together. Stitch around the rectangle perimeter using a ½" seam allowance, pivoting at the corners and leaving a 5" opening along one long edge for turning.
3. Turn the obi right side out. Press the edges, turning under the seam allowances at the opening. Topstitch around the obi perimeter, making sure to catch the opening edges.
4. Stitch buttons on both sides of the obi for fastening.

GRAPHIC Pillows

Graphic elements can add dimension and personality to otherwise basic pillows. Use a variety of shapes and contrasting fabrics to dress your furniture in sophisticated style.

Designed by Linda Lee

You'll Need
Yardages are based on 42"-wide fabric.
Materials listed make two 18"-square pillows.

- 1¼ yards of cotton velvet fabric
- ½ yard of contrasting silk doupioni
- 19" square of tagboard for circle pillow
- 2" x 10" strip of tagboard for square pillow
- Compass
- Sharp scissors to cut tagboard
- Chalk marker
- Double-sided fusible tape
- Matching all-purpose thread
- Turkish towel
- Two 18"-square pillow forms

Cutting

From the cotton velvet fabric, cut:

♦ 4 squares, 19" x 19"

From the silk doupioni, cut:

♦ 2 squares, 12" x 12"

Instructions

Use ½" seam allowances.

1. To create the template for the circle pillow, use a compass to draw an 8"-diameter circle centered on the 19" tagboard square. Cut out the circle and discard it. Place the tagboard template on one velvet square; use chalk to draw the circle onto the velvet.

2. Using a small stitch, staystitch the circle along the chalk line. Cut out the center of the circle, leaving a ½" seam allowance inside the chalk line. Clip the seam allowance to the staystitching every ½".

3. Place the velvet square, right side down, over the Turkish towel on an ironing surface. Position the tagboard cutout over the velvet square, matching the cut edges of the circle to the staystitching. Turn and press the clipped seam allowance over the edge of the tagboard.

4. Fuse small strips of double-sided fusible tape to the clipped seam allowance on the velvet-square wrong side. Remove the paper covering from the tape.

5. With right sides up, center the velvet square over a silk square. Place the Turkish towel over the velvet square; fuse the velvet square to the silk square, following the manufacturer's instructions.

6. Carefully fold the velvet square away from the silk square, exposing the staystitching on the circle. Using a zipper foot, stitch along the staystitching to secure the circle. This is the pillow-cover front.

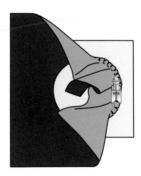

SEW SMART

You can also secure the circular opening by edgestitching close to the folded edge on the velvet square, or by slipstitching the folded edge by hand.

7. With right sides together, pin the pillow-cover front to a second velvet square. Stitch around the perimeter, pivoting at the corners and leaving a 7" opening on one edge for turning. Clip the corners to reduce the bulk.

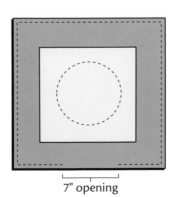

7" opening

8. Turn the pillow cover right side out, turning under the seam allowances at the opening. Insert the pillow form. Slipstitch the opening closed.

9. To construct the square pillow, draw a 7¼" square in the center of one velvet square. Using a small stitch, staystitch the square along the marked lines.

10. Cut out the square, leaving a ½" seam allowance inside the square. Discard the square. Clip the seam allowance to the staystitching in each corner.

11. Place the velvet square, right side down, over the Turkish towel on an ironing surface. Lay the 2" x 10" tagboard strip along one staystitching edge; turn and press the seam allowance over the tagboard edge. Repeat on the remaining edges.

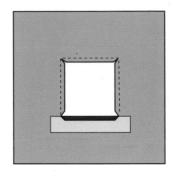

12. Fuse small strips of double-sided fusible tape to the seam allowances on the velvet-square wrong side. Remove the paper covering from the tape.

13. With right sides up, center the velvet square over the remaining silk square. Place the Turkish towel over the velvet square; fuse the velvet square to the silk square, following the manufacturer's instructions.

14. Carefully fold the velvet square away from the silk square along one edge, exposing the staystitching. Stitch barely to the left of the staystitching. Repeat for the remaining square edges to complete the pillow-cover front.

15. With right sides together, sew the pillow-cover front to the remaining velvet square, leaving a 7" opening on one edge for turning. Turn the pillow cover right side out and insert the pillow form. Turn under the seam allowances at the opening. Slipstitch the opening closed.

BUTTONED and BASIC Pillows

It's amazing how much a simple pillow can change the feel of a room. Just look through any decorating magazine or catalog to see the creative possibilities. Make the basic pillow for starters, and then add the buttoned version for a tailored touch. You'll be surprised at how easy they are—and you'll love the modest cost.

Designed by Gena Bloemendaal

You'll Need

*Yardages are based on 54"-wide fabric.
Materials listed make one 18" x 18" Basic Pillow
and one 16" x 16" Buttoned Pillow.*

For Basic Pillow
- ⅝ yard of decorator fabric
- Matching all-purpose thread
- One 18"-square pillow form

For Buttoned Pillow
- ½ yard of decorator fabric
- 4 buttons, 1" in diameter or desired size
- Matching all-purpose thread
- One 16"-square pillow form

VARY THE SIZE

Pillow forms come in all shapes and sizes. To determine the yardage for any basic pillow, add 1" to the pillow form height and width. Calculate the yardage based on two pieces cut to these measurements.

Basic Pillow Instructions

Use ½" seam allowances unless otherwise noted.

1. Cut two 19" squares.
2. With right sides together, stitch around the perimeter, pivoting at the corners and leaving a 7" opening on one edge for turning. Clip the corners to reduce the bulk.

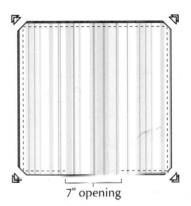

7" opening

3. Turn the pillow cover right side out, turning under the seam allowances at the opening. Insert the pillow form. Slipstitch the opening closed.

Buttoned Pillow Instructions

This tailored version is a variation on the basic pillow. Choose understated buttons for a subtle effect, or look for unique buttons that steal the show.

1. Cut one 12" x 17" rectangle and one 11" x 17" rectangle for the pillow-cover front. Cut one 17" square for the pillow-cover back.

2. On the 12" x 17" rectangle, turn under ½" to the wrong side on one long edge; stitch. Turn under another 2" to form the hem; stitch.

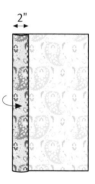

3. On the 11" x 17" rectangle, turn under ½" to the wrong side on one long edge; stitch. Turn under another ½" to form the hem; stitch.

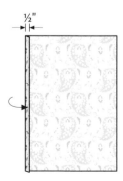

4. Measure and mark buttonhole positions on the piece with the deeper hem, placing the upper and lower buttonholes 4" from the raw edges and spacing the remaining two buttonholes 3" apart. Stitch and cut.

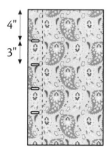

5. With right sides up and the rectangle with the buttonholes on top, overlap the two pieces so the width measures 17". Baste the edges through all layers.

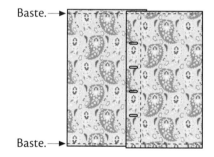

6. Mark the button positions on the piece underneath. Stitch the buttons in place. Fasten the buttons.

7. With the pillow-cover front and back pieces right sides together and using a ½" seam allowance, stitch around the perimeter, pivoting at the corners. Trim the corners to reduce the bulk. Press the edges to set the stitches.

8. Unfasten the buttons to turn the pillow cover right side out. Insert the pillow form. Fasten the buttons.

Sunroom SEATING

When you entertain alfresco this summer, surprise your guests with comfy and colorful pillows scattered on the outdoor furniture. Hundreds of durable fabrics are available for outdoor decor, ranging from the subdued colors of nature to bright stripes and charming prints.

Designed by Rhonda Darnell

You'll Need
Yardages are based on 54"-wide fabric. Materials listed make two 18" x 18" pillows and two 14" x 18" pillows.

♦ 1⅓ yards of blue-and-white striped fabric
♦ ⅝ yard of red-and-white striped fabric
♦ ⅝ yard of yellow-and-white striped fabric
♦ ⅝ yard of red print

♦ 2 yards of ⅜"-wide double-sided fusible tape for the Square Deal pillow
♦ Rotary cutter, ruler, and mat
♦ Yardstick
♦ Matching all-purpose thread
♦ Four 16"-long zippers
♦ Two 18"-square pillow forms
♦ Two 14" x 18" pillow forms

Square Deal: 18" x 18"

Square Deal Instructions

Use ½" seam allowances.

1. With the stripes running horizontally, cut a 21" square from the blue-and-white striped fabric, making sure to center the stripes from top to bottom precisely. Using a yardstick and a pencil, draw diagonal lines connecting the corners and forming four triangles. Cut the square carefully along the lines. Use the two triangles with the stripes parallel to the long edge; discard the other two.

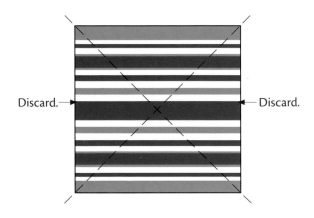

2. Using the retained triangles as patterns, place them on the remaining fabric. Carefully align the stripes and cut two more identical triangles.

3. Arrange the four triangles so the stripes form concentric squares.

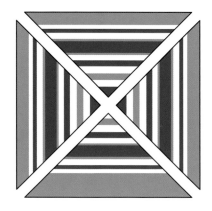

4. Working with two adjoining triangles, turn under and press a ½" seam allowance on one triangle where it will meet the other triangle. Press the ⅜" fusible tape to the turned-under seam allowance; remove the paper backing. With right sides facing up, place the turned-under edge over the second triangle as it will be sewn, carefully aligning all stripes and raw edges. Press to fuse the triangles.

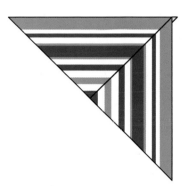

5. Carefully turn the triangles over so the wrong sides are facing up. Stitch exactly in the crease to form one half of the pillow-cover front. Repeat with the remaining two triangles.
6. Join the two pillow-front halves using the same process. The pillow front should measure 19" square when pieced.

7. Cut a 19" square for the back and install the zipper as described in "Zip Tips" at right.
8. See "Finishing" at right to complete the pillow.

ZIP TIPS

Follow these general instructions to add the zipper to each pillow style.
1. On the pillow-cover edges where the zipper will be installed, zigzag or serge to prevent fraying.
2. To insert the zipper, fold the pillow-cover front and back lower edges ½" to the wrong sides; press. Unfold the pressed edges and, with right sides together, stitch in the crease approximately 1½" from each end, leaving most of the edge open.
3. Attach the zipper foot to your sewing machine. With the front and back right side up, place the closed zipper under the opening, aligning the pillow-front folded edge with the lengthwise center of the zipper; pin. Stitch ¼" from the fabric edge along the zipper, backstitching at the start and finish; cut the thread. Rotate the project and position the pillow-back folded edge so it abuts the pillow-front folded edge; stitch the remaining side of the zipper.

FINISHING

Once the zipper is installed, open it halfway. With right sides together, pin the pillow-cover front and back along the remaining edges; stitch using a ½" seam allowance, pivoting at the corners. Clip the corners to reduce the bulk. Press the seams to set the stitches. Open the zipper and turn the pillow cover right side out; insert the pillow form and zip the pillow cover closed.

Pattern Play: 18" x 18"

Pattern Play Instructions

Use ½" seam allowances.

1. Using the rotary cutter, ruler, and mat, cut the pieces to the measurements shown. The pillow-cover front should measure 19" square when pieced; trim the side edges as needed.

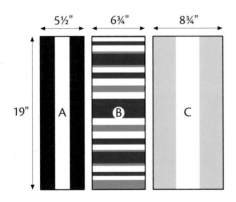

SEW SMART

To ensure that a full vertical stripe will show when two pieces are joined, plan to cut the striped fabric ½" *beyond* the stripe that will join to another piece. When stitching the pieces right sides together, sew with the striped fabric on top and use the stripe as a stitching guide.

2. With right sides together, pin piece A to piece B; stitch. Press the seam to set the stitches, and then press the seam allowances to one side.
3. With right sides together, stitch piece C to piece B in the same manner.
4. Cut a 19" square for the back and install the zipper as described in "Zip Tips" on page 75.
5. See "Finishing" on page 75 to complete the pillow.

Red, White, and Blue: 14" x 18"

Red, White, and Blue Instructions

Use ½" seam allowances.

1. Cut the striped pieces to the measurements shown below. The pillow-cover front should measure 15" x 19" when pieced.

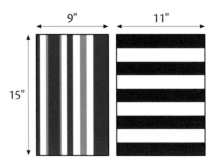

2. With right sides together, pin the two rectangles along the 15" edges; stitch. Press the seam to set the stitches, and then press the seam allowances to one side.
3. Cut a 15" x 19" rectangle for the back and install the zipper as described in "Zip Tips" on page 75.
4. See "Finishing" on page 75 to complete the pillow.

Red, White, and Yellow: 14" x 18"

Red, White, and Yellow Instructions

Use ½" seam allowances.

1. Cut the striped and print pieces to the measurements shown below. The pillow-cover front should measure 15" x 19" when pieced.

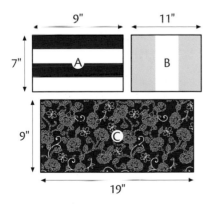

2. With right sides together, pin pieces A and B along the 7" edges; stitch. Press the seam to set the stitches, and then press the seam allowances to one side. With the joined section on top and right sides together, pin piece C to the joined section; stitch. Press the seam to set the stitches, and then press the seam allowances toward piece C.

3. Cut a 15" x 19" rectangle for the back and install the zipper as described in "Zip Tips" on page 75.

4. See "Finishing" on page 75 to complete the pillow.

Gather 'ROUND

Fabric yo-yos are typically used as charming little adornments for quilts, clothing, and more. Make an oversized yo-yo the main event by transforming it into a pillow. It's the perfect way to showcase two fabrics in one sunny cushion.

Designed by Diane Gilleland

You'll Need
Yardages are based on 42"-wide fabric.
Materials listed will make one 16" round pillow.

◆ 1 yard of mediumweight cotton fabric (fabric A)
◆ ⅝ yard of coordinating cotton fabric (fabric B)
◆ 6" square of fusible web
◆ Matching all-purpose thread
◆ Hand-sewing needle
◆ One 16" round pillow form

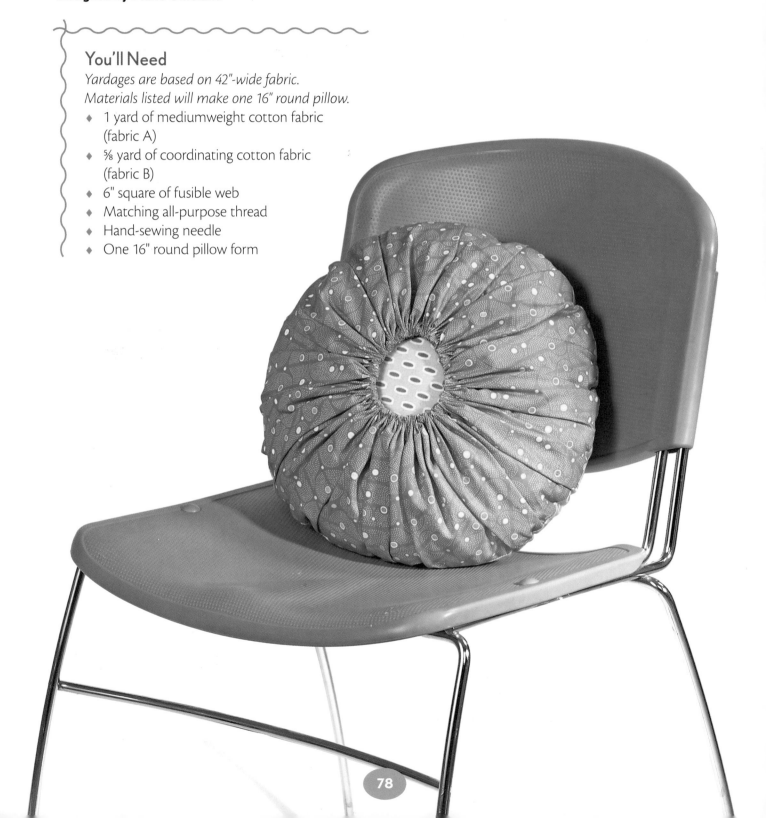

Instructions

1. From fabric A, cut a 32"-diameter circle.

SMOOTH SAILING

To create an even circle, begin with a 32" square. Fold it into quarters and round off the corners.

---

2. From fabric B, cut a 6"-diameter circle. Fuse the wrong side of the circle to the fusible web, following the manufacturer's instructions; trim the fusible web even with the circle. Fuse the fabric B circle to the wrong side of the fabric A circle.

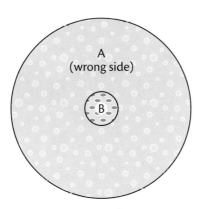

3. Fold the large circle edges ½" toward the wrong side; press. Thread a hand sewing needle with two long thread strands; knot the end. Hand stitch a running stitch around the circle, ¼" from the pressed edge.

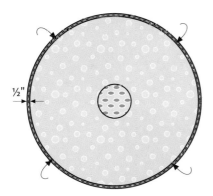

4. Pull the thread to gather the outer edge. Distribute the gathers along the thread and continue pulling until the circle forms a yo-yo with a 3" opening at the center. Tie off the thread.

SEW SMART

If you begin to run out of thread, pull the needle to gather the fabric and give you more thread to work with. The gathered seam should be stitched with one continuous thread.

---

5. Press the yo-yo edges flat to hold the circular shape.
6. Cut a 16½"-diameter circle from fabric B. With right sides together, pin this circle to the front of the yo-yo.
7. Stitch around the circle perimeter ¼" from the edge, leaving an 8" opening for turning. Clip the seam allowances every ¼" to reduce the bulk.

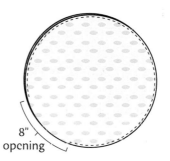

8" opening

8. Turn the pillow cover right side out; press. Insert the pillow form. Turn in the opening edges ¼". Slipstitch the opening closed.

YO-YO NOTES

Keep these yo-yo tips in mind when making this pillow or embellishing other projects.

- When stitching yo-yos, there isn't a substitute for hand sewing. Hand-sewn gathering stitches create a lovely ruffled edge, whereas a machine stitch leaves a clearly visible seamline.
- When making yo-yos in typical sizes (3" in diameter and smaller), begin with a circle that's twice as wide as the desired finished yo-yo size, plus a ½" seam allowance. The extra ½" makes a big difference because small yo-yos are gathered tightly in the center.

Connect the DOTS

A fuzzy fleece pillow covered in circle appliqués is sure to elicit *oohs* and *aahs* from houseguests.

Designed by Ellen March

You'll Need

Yardages are based on 54"- or 60"-wide fabric. Materials listed make one 18"-square pillow.

- ¾ yard of red fleece fabric
- ⅛ yard *each* of white and green fleece fabric
- Two 20" squares of adhesive-backed wash-away stabilizer
- All-purpose thread in red, white, and green
- 12"-long invisible zipper
- Invisible zipper foot
- One 18"-square pillow form
- Compass and water-soluble fabric-marking pen

Cutting

From the red fleece fabric, cut:

- 2 squares, 19" x 19"
- 10 circles, ¾" in diameter
- 10 circles, 1½" in diameter
- 10 circles, 2¼" in diameter

From *each* of the white and green fleece fabrics, cut:

- 10 circles, ¾" in diameter
- 10 circles, 1½" in diameter
- 10 circles, 2½" in diameter

Instructions

Use ½" seam allowances.

1. Position each fleece circle on one fleece square, overlapping the circles for a pleasing design. Use more or fewer circles depending on your preference. Leave ¾" of fabric free at the edges for side seam allowances and for room to maneuver the presser foot past the fleece circles.

2. Score the stabilizer paper backing on both squares and peel it away to expose the adhesive. Center one stabilizer square on the fleece square, sandwiching the circles. Hand-press lightly to adhere.

3. Position the stabilized fleece square on a work surface with the wrong side facing up. Center the remaining stabilizer square on the fleece square wrong side, matching the stabilizer edges. Hand-press lightly to adhere the layers.

4. With matching thread, edgestitch each circle through all the layers. Backstitch at the beginning and end of each stitching.

5. Using sharp, pointed scissors, cut away as much of the stabilizer as possible on either side of the stitching lines.

6. Wash away the remaining stabilizer, following the manufacturer's instructions. It may be necessary to soak the square overnight. Let the square dry thoroughly.

7. Install the invisible-zipper foot on the machine. Center one zipper-tape edge lengthwise along one fleece square edge. Stitch the zipper tape to the fleece square following the manufacturer's instructions, making sure the zipper coils are on the seamline.

8. Position the remaining fleece square over the embellished fleece square with right sides together and all edges and corners aligned; pin. Stitch the opposite zipper-tape edge to the corresponding fleece edge.

9. Switch to the regular zipper foot. Stitch the remainder of each seam beyond each zipper-tape end, getting your regular zipper foot as close as possible to the invisible zipper stitching. Open the zipper slightly. Stitch the remaining pillow-cover edges. Clip the corners to reduce the bulk.

10. Turn the pillow cover right side out through the zipper opening. Insert the pillow form; zip the pillow cover closed.

CUBE Pillow

Add a hip-to-be-square accent to your surroundings. A unique twist on a home-decorating staple, this clever 8" x 8" x 8" pillow will add a modern touch to any room in your home. A striped fabric is ideal for this angular shape.

Designed by Linda Lee

You'll Need

- ⅞ yard of cotton duck, lightweight denim, or decorator fabric
- 9"-long zipper
- Polyester fiberfill
- Matching all-purpose thread

Instructions

Use ½" seam allowances unless otherwise noted.

1. Measure, mark, and cut out the pillow cover according to the chart. Mark all letters and foldlines on the wrong side of fabric. See page 84 for cube pillow layout.

2. Staystitch the four inside corners along the seamlines. Clip into each corner, being careful not to cut the stitching. Also staystitch along the seamlines perpendicular to each foldline on the left and right "arms" of the piece. Clip to the staystitching at these foldlines. (Do *not* clip at the points A, B, C, and D.) Turn the end of the right arm 1" toward the wrong side; press to create a fold.

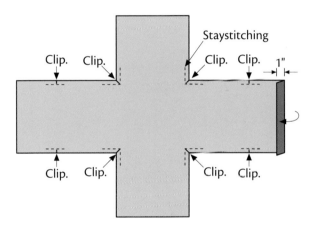

3. Open the zipper. With the zipper pull face down, align the zipper tape with the raw edge of the fabric at the folded end. Using a zipper foot, stitch close to the zipper teeth.

4. Turn the edge of the opposite arm ½" to the wrong side; press to create a fold. Bring that fold to meet the zipper, aligning the edge of the zipper tape with the raw edge of the fabric underneath. Stitch the zipper close to the zipper teeth.

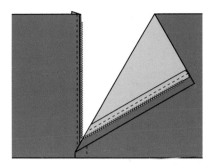

5. Close the zipper and allow the zipper placket to lie flat. With right sides together, fold the pillow cover, matching mark B to B, and mark C to C. Pivot the fabric at the foldline clips to match the E points on the upper edges. Stitch three sides of the pillow cover, putting the needle down at the clipped corners to raise the presser foot and pivot the work.

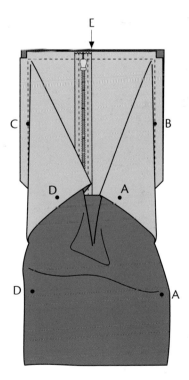

SHORTENING A ZIPPER

A 9"-long zipper is a tad long for this project, but the next shorter size is only 7" long. That's a bit too short for the job. However, you can make a 9"-long zipper work. Simply thread a hand-sewing needle and knot the two ends of thread together. Stitch multiple times by hand around the coils of the zipper where you'd like the zipper pull to stop, about 8" from the top of the zipper. Then using craft scissors, you can snip away the end of the zipper you don't need, leaving about ½" of zipper tape beyond your stitching.

6. Open the zipper. Repeat to sew the remaining sides of the pillow cover, matching points A, D, and E.
7. Reach through the open zipper to turn the pillow cover right side out.
8. Stuff the pillow cover with fiberfill, making sure to fill the corners to square up the shape. Zip the pillow closed.

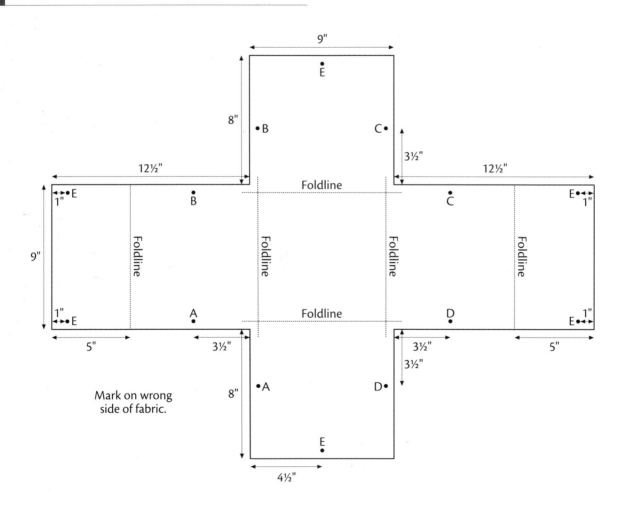

SHIRRED Pillows

Shirring creates instant texture and is easily done on a variety of fabrics. These pillows give you a chance to perfect your shirring skills while creating cool accents for your home. Make the pillows using smooth silk and luscious velvet as shown, or experiment with other fabrics.

Designed by Gena Bloemendaal

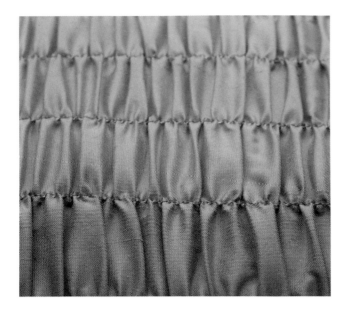

You'll Need

For Pink Pillow

Materials listed make one 16" x 16" pillow.

- 1⅛ yards of pink silk for pillow front
- ⅝ yard of embroidered pink silk for pillow back
- Acrylic ruler with marked grid
- White elastic thread
- Matching all-purpose thread
- Air- or water-soluble fabric-marking pen
- One 16"-square pillow form

For Chocolate Pillow

Materials listed make one 9" x 12" pillow.

- ¾ yard of chocolate brown stretch velvet
- Acrylic ruler with marked grid
- Black elastic thread
- Matching all-purpose thread
- Air- or water-soluble fabric-marking pen or tailor's chalk
- Polyester fiberfill

Pink Pillow Instructions

Use ½" seam allowances.

1. From the plain silk, cut one 36" square. From the embroidered silk, cut one 17" square and set it aside.

2. Press the plain silk square to remove wrinkles, using your iron's silk setting. Using the ruler and the fabric-marking pen, draw stitching lines across the fabric right side, spacing them 1" apart.

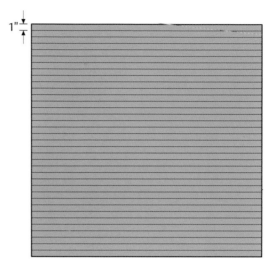

1"

3. Hand wind the elastic thread onto a bobbin, stretching the elastic slightly as you wind. Insert the bobbin in the machine and thread the needle with matching all-purpose thread. Set the machine for a 3.5 mm- or 4.0 mm-long stitch.

4. Stitch along each marked line; do not backstitch. Leave at least 3" of thread tails at each end. Tie the thread ends at the start and finish of each row of stitching. (Backstitching to secure when using elastic thread can be problematic, so we don't recommend it.)

5. Place the shirred fabric right side up on your ironing board. Hold a steam iron directly above the shirring and steam for approximately 10 seconds. Allow the fabric to cool, and then turn it over and repeat on the wrong side.

6. Measure and mark a 17" square on the shirred fabric. Stitch ⅛" *inside* the marked square to secure the shirring. Trim the square on the marked lines.

7. With right sides together, stitch the shirred square and the embroidered square, leaving an 8" opening on one edge for turning. Clip the corners to reduce the bulk.

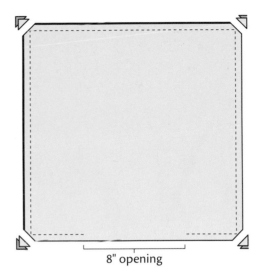

8" opening

8. Turn the pillow cover right side out, turning under the seam allowances at the opening. Insert the pillow form. Slipstitch the opening closed.

PILLOW PLAY
For all you free spirits out there, play with changing the spacing between stitching lines and see what happens.

Chocolate Pillow Instructions
Use ½" seam allowances.
1. From the stretch velvet, cut one 22" x 28" rectangle and one 10" x 13" rectangle. Set the 10" x 13" rectangle aside.

2. Press the 22" x 28" rectangle carefully to remove wrinkles. Working on the fabric right side, measure and pin-mark a centered 6" section. Using a ruler and the fabric-marking pen or tailor's chalk, draw stitching lines across the 6" section, spacing them 1½" apart.

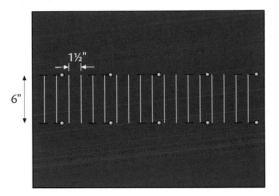

3. Hand wind the elastic thread onto a bobbin, stretching the elastic slightly as you wind. Insert the bobbin in the machine, and thread the needle with matching all-purpose thread. Set the machine for a 3.5 mm- or 4.0 mm-long stitch.
4. Stitch along each marked line; do not backstitch. Leave at least 3" of thread tails at each seam end. Pull the thread ends to the wrong side at the start and finish of each row of stitching and tie.
5. Place the shirred fabric right side up on your ironing board. Hold a steam iron directly above the shirring and steam for approximately 10 seconds. Allow the fabric to cool, and then turn it over and repeat on the wrong side.
6. Measure and mark a 10" x 13" rectangle on the shirred fabric, centering the shirred section. Stitch ⅛" *inside* the marked rectangle to secure the shirring. Trim the rectangle on the marked lines.
7. With right sides together, stitch the shirred rectangle and the remaining velvet rectangle, leaving a 6" opening on one long edge for turning. Clip the corners to reduce the bulk.
8. Turn the pillow cover right side out, turning under the seam allowances at the opening. Stuff the pillow with fiberfill. Slipstitch the opening closed.

ENVELOPE Pillow

This clever pillow is great for showcasing a beautiful fabric. Using a chopstick as a closure gives the pillow a unique twist.

Designed by Linda Lee

You'll Need

Materials listed make one 12" x 16" pillow.

- ⅝ yard of nondirectional print *or* 1⅛ yards of directional print (see "Home-Sewing Glossary" on page 95)
- ½ yard of contrasting fabric for overlap facing
- 1 yard of pattern paper
- Tailor's chalk
- Matching all-purpose thread
- 2" of ½"-wide elastic
- 1 chopstick
- One 12" x 16" pillow form

Pattern Instructions

Refer to the illustration below as a guide for making the pattern.

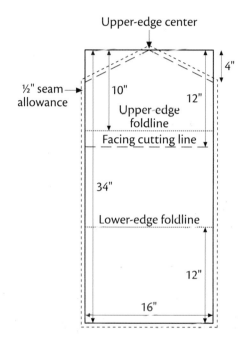

1. Draw a 16" x 34" rectangle on the pattern paper. Mark the upper-edge center.
2. Mark a point on each side edge 4" down from each upper corner. Draw diagonal lines from the upper-edge center to each side point to create the overlap cutting lines.
3. Draw a horizontal line 10" from the upper edge for the overlap foldline. Draw a horizontal line 12" from the upper edge to create a cutting line for the overlap facing.
4. Draw a horizontal line 12" from the lower edge for the lower foldline.
5. Add ½" to each outer edge for seam allowances.
6. Cut one pillow-cover piece from the fabric. Use tailor's chalk to transfer the foldlines onto the fabric.

7. Cut one overlap facing piece from the contrasting fabric, using the facing cutting line on the pattern.

Sewing Instructions

Use ½" seam allowances.

1. Finish the pillow-cover lower edge (see "A Fine Finish" below right). Press the finished edge ½" toward the wrong side; stitch.

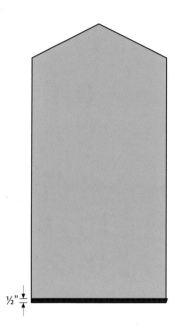

½"

2. With right sides together, fold the pillow-cover lower edge along the foldline and pin at the sides.

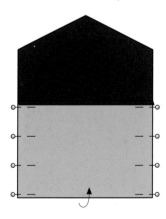

3. Finish the overlap-facing lower edge. With right sides together, position the facing on the pillow cover, lapping the facing over the pillow-cover hemmed edge; pin. Stitch the side seams and the overlap edges. Finish the edges.

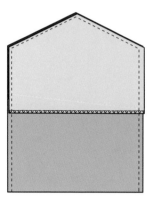

A FINE FINISH

Finish the raw edges of this pillow with one of the following methods: use pinking shears, zigzag the edges on the sewing machine, or overlock them using a serger.

4. Turn the pillow cover right side out. Press the overlap edges so the facing fabric doesn't show.

5. Mark a ¾" horizontal buttonhole 3½" from the point, centering it on the overlap. Stitch the buttonhole and cut it open.

6. Insert the pillow form. Position the overlap where you want it. Poke pins through the buttonhole to mark the placement of the elastic loop.

7. Remove the pillow form. Wrap the elastic around the chopstick to determine how much is required for the loop. Add enough to the loop length to sew it to the pillow cover. Hand tack or machine stitch the loop ends to the pillow cover.

8. Insert the pillow form again. Bring the elastic loop through the buttonhole and slip the chopstick through the loop.

Home-Sewing Specifications

This handy reference section offers simple, concise information to make your projects easier and more fun to sew.

Helpful Measurements

If you're making any project for a bed, such as trimmed sheets or a bed skirt, it helps to know the standard dimensions of mattresses and sheets.

Mattress Sizes

Twin	39" x 75"
Twin XL	39" x 80"
Full	54" x 75"
Queen	60" x 80"
King	76" x 80"

Sheet Sizes

Twin	66" x 96"
Twin XL	66" x 102"
Full	81" x 96"
Queen	90" x 102"
King	108" x 102"

Standard pillowcases: 20" x 26"

Sewing a French Seam

This seam finish keeps sheer fabrics from raveling and makes the inside of your project look just as nice as the outside. If you choose to use this technique, base your cutting on a ⅝" seam allowance.

1. With *wrong* sides together, pin the pieces along the edges. Stitch using a ¼" seam allowance; trim the seam allowances to ⅛". Press the seam to set the stitches, and then press the seam allowances to one side.

2. Pick up the joined pieces from the wrong side and fold the fabric at the seamline, right sides together, encasing the narrow seam allowances. Stitch using a ⅜" seam allowance. Press the finished seam allowance to one side.

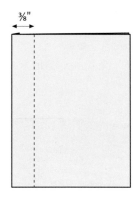

Sewing a Slipstitch

This stitch is useful when sewing by machine is difficult or too obvious, such as closing the openings on pillow covers.

Pick up a thread or two of the fabric, and then slide the needle through the folded edge, traveling ⅛" to ¼" before taking the next stitch.

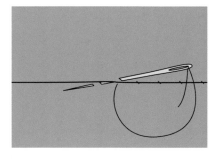

Matching a Pattern Repeat

When you're making a project like the tab curtains on page 47, pattern repeat (the vertical distance from one element of the pattern to the next identical element) may come into play. If your fabric has a small-scale allover design, you don't need to consider pattern repeat. But if your fabric has a prominent motif that recurs at a set interval, you'll want those motifs to fall in the same spot on both curtain panels.

Here's the formula for determining how much yardage you'll need:

1. Start with the cut length of the curtain panels. In "Room with a View" on page 47, the cut length of each curtain panel is 64".
2. Measure the pattern repeat in the fabric you're considering. Add that measurement to the cut length to arrive at the total length needed for one panel.
3. Multiply the total length by 2, the number of panels needed for this project.
4. Divide the total number of inches by 36 inches to arrive at the yardage needed.
5. Round the yardage needed up to the nearest ¼ yard.

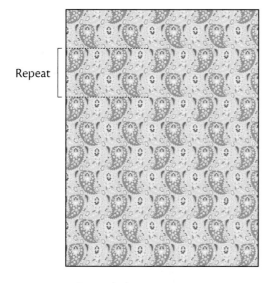

Repeat

Hand Embroidery

Learn the basic stitches and you can create beautiful hand-embroidered items.

You'll Need

There are lots of fun hand-embroidery supplies available—some are so cool, you'll want them just to decorate your sewing room! Here's what you need to start embroidering by hand.

Hoops are made of metal, plastic, or wood, and come in different sizes and colors. They hold the fabric taut while you sew, ensuring even stitches.

Embroidery floss is made up of six loosely twisted

strands and comes in a coil called a skein. Experiment with cotton, rayon, or silk varieties that have different sheens.

Embroidery needles, or crewel needles, have a long eye to accommodate several strands of floss—the smaller the size, the longer the needle. Use a large size for heavyweight fabrics and a small size for lightweight fabrics.

Embroidery transfers are paper patterns that are "transferred" to fabric by heat from an iron. Using a transfer is much easier than creating the design from scratch!

Embroidery scissors are often 3½" to 4½" long to ensure proper clipping of even the smallest threads.

Aida fabric, a cotton fabric with woven threads, is commonly used for cross-stitching. Aida fabric is also available in linen, rayon/cotton blends, or polyester/cotton blends and in different sizes: 11-, 14-, 16-, and 18-count (holes per inch). Use any fabric you like for hand embroidery, but make sure the print (if you're using one) won't compete with your design.

Embroidery Stitches

Blanket stitch. The blanket stitch is worked from left to right over two imaginary lines. Bring the thread up at 1 and down at 2. Bring the thread up at 3, catching the thread from the first stitch. Repeat.

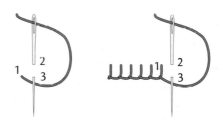

Chain stitch. See page 10.
Couching stitch. Position the surface thread, trim, or floss on the fabric right side. Bring the couching thread up from the fabric wrong side using a large-eyed needle. Take a small, straight stitch over the surface thread at 1 and back through the fabric at 2.

Cross-stitch. The cross-stitch is made by two bisecting diagonal stitches. Bring the needle up to the fabric right side at 1 and back through at 2, and then up again at 3, and down again at 4. Repeat. Following the opposite direction, bring the needle up through the fabric at 5, and then back down at 6. Repeat.

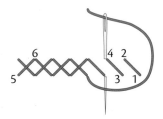

Fly stitch. Also known as the "Y" stitch, or open-loop stitch, the fly stitch is a V-shaped loop that's tied down with a vertical straight stitch. Bring the needle up at 1. Hold a bit of floss down with your thumb and insert the needle at 2. Take a small stitch along the center of the V at 3. Pull it through the fabric and secure it in position with a small loop.

French knot. See page 10.

Lazy daisy stitch. Bring the needle up from the fabric wrong side at 1 and hold the thread with your thumb. Insert the needle back into where it first came out at 2, and then guide the needle back through the fabric a small distance from the center at 3. With the thread wrapped under the needle point, pull the needle through the fabric; fasten the loop with a small stitch. To make a flower, stitch in a circle with each stitch radiating outward to form petals.

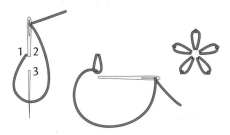

Leaf (feather) stitch. Bring the needle up from the fabric wrong side at 1 and hold the thread down with your thumb. Insert the needle a little to the right of the invisible line at 2 and take a small stitch

in a downward diagonal motion so that the needle point appears on the centerline. Keeping the thread under the needle point, pull the thread through the fabric at 3. Make a second stitch in the same manner. Insert the needle a little to the left and make a small diagonal stitch so that the needle point comes out on the centerline. Keep the thread under the needle point; pull the thread through the fabric to make the stitch. Repeat the stitch, alternating from side to side.

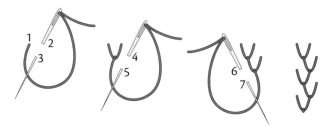

Running stitch. Bring the thread up from the wrong side at 1. Insert the needle at 2, up at 3, in at 4, and up at 5. Pull the thread through. Keep the stitches about twice as long as the spaces between them. Knot the thread on the wrong side at the end of the last stitch.

Split stitch. Bring the thread up from the fabric wrong side and take a stitch through the fabric. Point the needle backward along the line and stitch through the thread loop of the previous stitch.

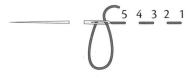

Stem stitch. Working from left to right, bring the floss up from the fabric wrong side at 1. Take a straight stitch, leaving the needle on the fabric wrong side at 2. Bring the needle to the fabric right side, slightly to the right of where it first emerged at 3.

HOME-SEWING GLOSSARY

Appliqué	Shape cut from fabric and applied to another surface
Baste	Long, temporary stitches that hold two or more layers of fabric together; can be done by hand or machine
Batting	Made of polyester, polyester/cotton, cotton, wool, or silk, it's the middle layer in bed coverings that gives the cover loft. Also often used for smaller projects, like place mats.
Bias	Diagonal fabric grain; ideal for piping and binding because it curves smoothly
Box Pleat	Pleating technique that folds fabric in opposite directions so they meet in the middle
Clip	Short cut into a seam allowance around curves or into corners to create ease
Directional Print	Patterned fabric with a definite up-and-down design, requiring that you cut pieces in the same direction
Drop	Distance from table or mattress edge to finished edge
Fabric Width	Fabric measurement from selvage to selvage
Fiberfill	Loose polyester or other material used for stuffing
Finger-Press	Technique of pressing small fabric sections without an iron; fabrics are flattened between thumb and forefinger
Fullness	Allowance for gathers, usually 2 to 3 times the window width, or pillow or tablecloth perimeter
Gimp	Narrow braid used to cover exposed seams; also can be used as embellishment
Grainline	Directions of threads that make up fabric; lengthwise grain threads are parallel to selvage and crosswise grain threads are at right angles to selvage
Miter	Angle formed at a corner for a neat finish
Nondirectional Print	Patterned fabric that appears the same in each direction, making it possible to cut pieces lengthwise or crosswise
Pattern Repeat	Distance between same design or motif on fabric
Piping	Fabric-covered cording with lip for insertion in a seam; may also be "flat," without cording
Seam Allowance	Distance from stitching line to fabric edge; usually ½" for home-decorating projects
Selvage	Finished edge on woven fabrics
Slipstitch	A nearly invisible stitch for closing the opening on a pillow cover or table runner; see page 92
Soutache	A narrow flat braid in a herringbone pattern used for trimming edges and embroidery
Staystitch	Straight line of machine stitching inside seam allowance, used to stabilize a curved or bias edge
Usable Fabric Width	Actual fabric area that can be used, excluding selvages; not always complete fabric width

Project CONTRIBUTORS

Pamela K. Archer lives, sews, and teaches in the greater Portland, Oregon, area. A longtime fiber fanatic, Pam shares her love of sewing through classes and freelance writing for several sewing publications. She's the author of *Fast, Fun and Easy Fabric Bags* and *Fast, Fun and Easy Home Accents*.

Kate Bashynski received a bachelor of arts in fashion design from Mount Mary College, in Milwaukee, Wisconsin. In 1996 she began working at Nancy's Notions as part of the PBS *Sewing With Nancy* team. Machine embroidery has brought additional creative outlets for Kate in designing embroidered compositions on fabric and clothing, as well as creating embroidery collections. She resides near Randolph, Wisconsin, with her husband and their dog.

Gena Bloemendaal is a former *Sew News* editor who is living out her dream job of being a mom. She's also a freelance writer and photographer, and she continues to sew professionally and for her own enjoyment. Her latest hobby: updating her home with sewing projects that reflect her own style and personality.

Beth Bradley has always been fascinated by fashion. She learned to sew in high school and went on to earn a degree in apparel design and production. Beth is currently the associate editor of *Sew News* magazine.

Rhonda Darnell sews from her California home to create custom interior projects. Her other passions are decorating, crafting, gardening, traveling, and writing about all of the above. She especially enjoys trips to Europe with her family and is slowly redecorating her home to reflect her love of all things French.

Shannon Dennis is currently an independent author and professed omni-crafter living in Cleveland, Ohio. She's the founder of Nina (www.theninaline.com) and writes for a number of print and online publications.

Sandra Geiger began sewing when she was a child. She lives in Wisconsin, and has owned a quilt shop and taught sewing as a 4-H instructor. Sandra also taught her daughter Sara Boughner, another *Sew News* contributor, how to sew.

Diane Gilleland produces CraftyPod, a blog and podcast about all things crafty (www.craftypod.com). Her first book is *Kanzashi in Bloom*, from Watson-Guptill, and is available at www.randomhouse.com.

Debbie Homer began sewing as a child on the family farm in rural Idaho, and it has been a lifetime passion for her. She also has years of experience as an educator for RNK Distributing. Visit rnkdistributing.com to see the entire line of products and to get free sewing and embroidery projects.

Cindy Kacynski is a freelance writer, serging expert, and hobbyist who enjoys sewing, decorating, scrapbooking, and photography. She lives in Superior, Colorado, with her husband and two daughters.

Linda Lee is the owner of The Sewing Workshop Pattern Collection, a group of patterns for distinctive garments using innovative sewing techniques. A licensed interior designer and member of ASID since 1974, Linda has written 13 books. Visit www.sewingworkshop.com for more information.

Ellen March has sewing in her blood. At 16, she starred in the educational film *Picking Your Pattern, Fabric and Notions*, and she has since appeared on DIY's *Uncommon Threads* and on PBS's *MacPhee Workshop*. Ellen is currently the editor-in-chief of *Sew News*, *Sew It All*, and *Creative Machine Embroidery* magazines.

Shannon Okey is the author of over 10 fabric- and fiber-related books, including the thrift-store-makeover sewing book *AlterNation* and of course, *The Pillow Book*. She is a columnist for *knit.1* magazine and has appeared on many crafty television shows. Find her online at www.knitgrrl.com.

Linda Permann is an avid sewer, quilter, crocheter, and crafter. She's designed projects for a number of books and magazines and was the founding Craft and Decorating editor of *Adorn* magazine. She blogs about sewing, crafts, and living in Montana at www.lindamade.com/wordpress.

Lisa Shepherd Stewart is an author and designer specializing in African fabrics for sewing, decorating, and quilting. Her third book, *African Accents ON THE GO! Designing Accessories with Cultural Style*, features 22 original handbag, tote, and take-along projects to sew. Visit www.culturedexpressions.com.

Marla Stefanelli is a former costumer and graphic designer turned snowboarder. She takes a break from her hectic schedule to create and explain in no-nonsense terms how to create fabulous projects.